Hitler

Hitler

Profile of a Dictator

David Welch

London and New York

First published 1998 by UCL Press

This edition first published 2001
by Routledge
11 New Fetter Lane, London EC4P 4EE

Simultaneously published in the USA and Canada
by Routledge
29 West 35th Street, New York, NY 10001

Routledge is an imprint of the Taylor & Francis Group

©1998, 2001 David Welch

Typeset in Sabon and Gill Sans by
Wilmaset Ltd, Birkenhead, Wirral
Printed and bound in Great Britain by
T. J. International, Padstow, UK

British Library Cataloguing-in-Publication Data
A catalogue record for this book is available from the British Library

Library of Congress Cataloging in Publication Data
A catalog record for this book has been requested

ISBN 0–415–25074–9 (Hbk)
ISBN 0–415–25075–7 (Pbk)

Contents

Acknowledgements

I am indebted to many individuals in the preparation of this work. Special thanks are due to my family, friends and colleagues for their encouragement and support. I would like in particular to thank Professor Jeremy Noakes who read and made valuable comments on the manuscript.

Finally, I would like to thank successive generations of "Special Subject" students at Canterbury who have taken my "Life in the Third Reich" course and who have (by and large!) helped shape and refine my own ideas through their own engagement with the topic. My research students over the years have extended my knowledge still further. Since the appearance of the first edition in 1998 the historiography of the Third Reich and on Hitler in particular has continued unabated. This new edition incorporates the most important recent publication and the bibliography has been updated to reflect new scholarship.

David Welch
Canterbury
September 2000

Introduction

"Not another book on Hitler!" I can hear you say. Yes, this is another book on Hitler, but it is most certainly not another biography. Ian Kershaw, who has written widely on Hitler, has claimed that, "As Dictator of Germany, Hitler is for the historian largely unreachable, cocooned in the silence of the sources" (Kershaw 1993: 4) Kershaw was referring to the deliberate destruction of evidence by the Nazis towards the end of the war and the huge void in the sphere of central decision-making left by Hitler's extraordinary, unbureaucratic style of rule. I should like to turn the phrase round and state that, undeterred by Kershaw's warning, my intention in writing this book is to reach parts of Hitler that other historians have not reached! Put simply, the aim of the book is to try to clarify and elucidate Hitler's role within the rise and fall of the Third Reich.

By any stretch of the imagination Hitler's rise and fall was extraordinary. He was not an intellectual. He produced no great works of philosophy or art. He was not a military leader of genius or insight and yet this petit-bourgeois Austrian came to power constitutionally in 1933, he remained in power for 12 years and by 1941 he commanded a European empire not seen since the days of Napoleon. He was also the instigator of a genocidal war of unparalleled scope and brutality. How can the Hitler phenomenon be explained and, indeed, does it have any relevance over 50 years after his death? The publicity accorded in 1995 to the fiftieth anniversary of the collapse of the Third Reich and the death of its leader Adolf Hitler testifies to the undiminishing fascination with Nazism and the individual figure of Hitler. The two are inexorably linked both historically and in the manner in which they developed once in power. The historian

1

K.D. Bracher has even asserted that Hitler's personality is almost "totally submerged in the history of his political movement and the Third Reich" (Bracher 1979: 212). This interest has surely something to do with the general public's readiness to see the past in terms of the "history of great men". "Can we call him great?" asked Joachim Fest, one of Hitler's biographers. In terms of personality Hitler was a quite unremarkable and unlovely man. But his historical impact has been immense. The word most commonly associated with Hitler is "evil" and commentators have been quick to emphasize his role and personal responsibility for the undeniable crimes committed by the Nazi regime. Invariably Hitler is seen as a man who achieved power through the exercise of his own demonic will. Albert Speer's view that he was an "inexplicable demonic figure" that occurs only rarely in history is still widely shared. Indeed many of his biographers have sustained this view. Was Hitler 'truly evil'? Was he mad? He unquestionably possessed the 'virtue' of being without pity – even when compassion was asked of him. However to refer to Hitler as evil presupposes a moral judgement, but does not provide an explanation to questions such as why he hated the Jews so much he tried to kill them all. The continuing public obsession with Hitler's personality (and sexuality) has resulted also in a widening gap between popular and scholarly views of Hitler. While most historians would agree on the centrality of Hitler to the phenomenon of Nazism, locating Hitler's precise role within the Third Reich has proved controversial.

I have tried to tackle questions central to an understanding of National Socialism by focusing on the personality of Hitler, his ideas and the nature of his power. What was the appeal of Nazism and how far was its growing popularity in the Weimar Republic due to Hitler? What was the basis of Hitler's authority once in power and how responsible was Hitler for the shaping of policy? Was this authority eroded during the course of the Third Reich? What role did Hitler play in bringing about the Second World War? How great was the support for and opposition to Hitler and where did responsibility lie for the Holocaust?

How can we explain the rise of an individual whose political career had not begun until the age of 30 (in fact, Hitler continued to remain on the periphery of German politics until his fortieth birthday) yet who emerged from provincial obscurity to become Führer (leader) of the greatest military power in Europe, only to end as a charred corpse soaked in petrol? Sebastian Haffner claimed that Hitler "subordinated history to autobiography". Unquestionably a "conviction politician" in contemporary terminology, was Hitler a "conscious modernizer" with a programme for a revolutionary restructuring of society? Hitler was deeply anti-Marxist, but was he a revolutionary as well? Rainer Zitelmann's controversial biography written in the late 1980s claimed that Hitler was a leader who spoke in "utopian visions" and that these visionary goals of national resurgence constitute an underlying revolutionary mentality. Some historians argue that there is little that distinguished Hitler's brand of nationalistic politics from existing right-wing, Pan-German parties. Others have suggested that what separated Hitler from such groups was the creation of a unique "People's Community" (*Volksgemeinschaft*) based on race and struggle in which old conflicts would be forgotten.

Locating Hitler's role in the Third Reich has become the source of a major and sometimes acrimonious historiographical conflict. This has become known as the "intentionalist" versus "functionalist" debate. Briefly this may be summarized as the division of historians into "intentionalists" like K.D. Bracher and Klaus Hildebrand, who seek to emphasize Hitler's role in forming Nazi policy and the consistency of his ideas and leadership, and the "structural-functionalists", including Martin Broszat, Hans Mommsen and Wolfgang Schieder, who see developments during the Third Reich as the outcome of power groupings, largely uncoordinated, shaping policy. The recent move away from the "intentionalist" explanation has tended to downgrade the importance of Hitler and stress the "structural" constraints on policy and the chaotic nature of decision-making. The "structuralists" do not deny the centrality of the Führer to the phenomenon of Nazism, rather they focus on the structural context of decision making and the role of "traditional elites" in running the Third Reich and Hitler's inability (or unwillingness) to keep this chaos in check. Thus Hitler, in Hans Mommsen's famous phrase, was in some respects a "weak dictator" (Mommsen 1966: 98).

In the first chapter, on Hitler as "the young ideologue", I have attempted to reappraise Hitler's early speeches and writings to discover whether they provide insights into the nature of Nazism and go some way to answering the fundamental questions that I have raised above. For too long there has been a reluctance by historians to analyze personality in favour of "structures" of Nazism. This book is not, however, intended to be a traditional biography of the "great men in history" genre. We have witnessed a spate of such books in recent years. Nor have I employed a psychoanalytical assessment of Hitler's character and habits – psycho-historical techniques have rarely advanced our understanding of Hitler and Nazism. I am reminded of William Carr's admonition that works classed as psycho-historical "turn out all too often to be written by psychiatrists without any historical training or by historians primed with psycho-historical jargon" (Carr 1978: 473). Stated simply, my aim is to deduce Hitler's intentions from his speeches, his writings and his actions, to analyze the mechanisms by which he put his ideas into practice and to locate Hitler's precise role in the decision-making process of the Third Reich. This book is not intended to provide a detailed insight into Hitler's private life or the inner psychology but is concerned about the nature of Hitler's power – how he gained power, how he used power, and how he was allowed to abuse power by all the people around him. To answer such questions it is imperative to place Hitler's thoughts and actions in the wider perspective of German politics and society at that time. I would hope to offer a synthesis of intention and structure in explaining the manner in which Hitler was one element among many in a highly complex decision-making structure, which influenced him almost as much as he imposed his influence over it. Hitler's ideas and intentions were crucial for policy-making during the Third Reich, but the conditions under which these intentions became reality were not totally controlled by Hitler.

CHAPTER ONE

The young ideologue

There was nothing inevitable about the triumph of Adolf Hitler and his party the NSDAP. His rise to power was perfectly resistible. His early life provides little indication of a precocious talent or of the demagogic leader who was to have such a profound impact on the world stage. In 1923 when he was jailed for the abortive Munich *Putsch* the Bavarian authorities ought to have imprisoned him for longer and on his release he should have been deported to Austria. Had this happened it is very difficult to see how he could have resurrected his political career. He would have been finished as a political figure in Germany. Moreover, as late as 1928, Hitler and the Nazis were still peripheral political forces and in the elections of that year were rejected by 97 per cent of the electorate. Even when he was appointed Chancellor in March 1933, 56 per cent of voters still rejected him.

In order to understand Hitler's personal motivation and the psychological forces that propelled it, I have constructed this chapter around the six formative stages in Hitler's early political career. First there are the years 1904–6, his final years of school in Linz; secondly the formative political years in Vienna, 1907–13; thirdly, the experience of the Great War and the traumatic defeat of Germany; fourthly, the post-war period up to 1923 in Munich which resulted in the formation of the NSDAP and the abortive Munich *Putsch*; fifthly, the brief period of imprisonment in 1924 in Landsberg where he dictated *Mein Kampf* (*My struggle*); and finally, the ensuing years of political consolidation for both Hitler and the NSDAP culminating in electoral victory and the appointment of Hitler as Chancellor and "Führer" of Germany.

To understand Hitler's rise we need to look first at the man and his ideas. Ian Kershaw, who has subjected Hitler to considerable scrutiny, has warned that we should not overrate Hitler's personality as a factor in his power (Kershaw 1991: 16). What do we know about the man as opposed to the demagogue? Physically and intellectually he was unremarkable. He was of medium height. His somewhat stooped body was dominated by a large head featuring stern, unblinking eyes, a long nose and a trimmed moustache that has become synonymous with Hitler and used by cartoonists the world over. Photographic and film records reveal a mean, unforgiving face with little trace of humour or kindness. In his early political years he retained a dishevelled look, habitually wearing a dirty trench coat or raincoat and apparently caring little about his personal appearance (referred to by his biographer, Alan Bullock, as "a touch of Austrian *Schlamperei*"). On the other hand he retained a fetish for cleanliness and washing – psychologists have made much of this in analyzing a repressed, obsessive personality. He disliked work, was disorganized and incapable of personal discipline, and tended to live the life of listless bohemian pleasure. However, contemporaries noted that he was capable of stirring himself over an issue or an event that captured his imagination (Kubizek 1955). Although he liked the company of women there is no evidence during this period of his life of a long-term relationship or of sexual liaisons with the opposite sex (or indeed his own sex). He did not smoke, he rarely drank alcohol and (from the early 1930s onwards) he was a vegetarian. His passions were reading and talking (not debating) politics, listening to Wagner and watching films (one Christmas, for example, Goebbels' present to Hitler consisted of 30 serious films and 18 Mickey Mouse films). Hitler read widely though unsystematically. He possessed a prodigious memory and his tastes included the philosopher Nietzsche, Karl May, a writer of Westerns, and works on medicine, biology, astrology and occultism. Each in turn would excite him but he was incapable of sustaining intellectual curiosity in any single field. Nevertheless, he considered himself an expert on history, art and architecture. Commenting on reading in *Mein Kampf*, Hitler wrote: "Reading is not an end in itself, but a means to an end ... One who has cultivated the art of reading will instantly discern, in a book or journal or pamphlet, what ought to be remembered because it meets one's personal needs or is of value as general knowledge" (Hitler 1939: 42–3).

Although it cannot be denied that Hitler possessed a sharp-witted intelligence, it is equally clear that Hitler attempted to convey the impression of wider learning than, in fact, he possessed. As a boy his formal education had been disrupted and his reliance on self-learning went hand in hand with his contempt for "intellectuals'" and formal education. Hitler was a man with a closed mind for whom reading was a means of reinforcing his own prejudices. A.J.P. Taylor perceptively noted, for example, that he was not a close student of Nietzsche; it would be nearer the truth to say that he translated Wagner into political terms (Taylor 1979: 201). The shadowy figure that emerges from his time in Vienna is a selfish, frustrated, distant, unapproachable, lonely young man unloved and unloving, a man convinced of his superior abilities but frustrated that they were not recognized by others.

To the end of his life it is difficult to conceive of Hitler having a friend. Perhaps the closest was the architect and later Armaments Minister, Albert Speer. Interestingly enough, Speer never allowed himself to feel that he was Hitler's "friend", for, according to Speer, friendship requires mutual warmth that Hitler was incapable of giving. In conversation with Gitta Sereny, Speer confirmed that while he "enjoyed living in [Hitler's] aura of reflected glory" they never consciously thought of each other with affection. Sereny has speculated that Hitler was bedevilled from childhood by thwarted, imagined and withheld love – "a deficiency which rendered [him] virtually incapable of expressing private emotions ... though surrounded by people, [he] remained alone" (Sereny 1995: 102, 13).

What marks the young Hitler from the crowd is the extraordinary strength of his political convictions and his unwavering belief in his own rightness and destiny. The combination of "evangelical" zeal and vision partially explains his opaque philosophy and why he could not accept criticism or alternative proposals. For Hitler (and his followers) there could only be one path for the Nazi movement and for Germany. Hitler was not an original thinker. He drew upon a fund of ideas that he had gleaned from his eclectic reading as a boy and his time in Vienna (referred to by Sternburg as a 'nonsensical porridge of ideas' (Sternburg, 1996, p. 52)) and later as a soldier in the First World War. Hajo Holborn perceptively suggested that Hitler possessed 'an unkempt and primitive mind that lacked the power of discrimination but excelled in reducing simple ideas to even simpler terms while believing thereby to have achieved higher wisdom' (Holborn, 1952: 542ff.). Recent studies have tended to confirm that Hitler's personal worldview was neither a hotchpotch of racial nonsense nor merely a missionary desire to secure an electoral victory prior to 1933. What is incontestable is that the young Adolf Hitler drew upon a well-established German tradition for four of his main ideas: his unshakeable belief in the superiority of the German race and particularly of Aryans; his utter contempt for parliamentary democracy; his belief in the heroic leader figure; and his vehement anti-Semitism. (If one adds a strident nationalism, a hatred of equality and peace and a belief in the heroic virtues of war then we can identify the emergence of a full-blown fascist ideology.) Such ideas were in fact based upon various strands of intellectual thought which date back at least a century and which constitute the *völkisch* doctrine, which was essentially a product of late-eighteenth-century Romanticism. The major themes that recur in Hitler's *Weltanschauung* (worldview) reflect the roots and antecedents of *völkisch* (nationalist/racist) thought. Hitler's ideas – or more accurately, his "utopian visions" – were therefore entirely unoriginal. The originality was in Hitler's ability to mobilize a mass movement and eventually secure power on the basis of these ideas.

Adolf Hitler was born in Braunau am Inn, Austria, (on the Austrian border with Germany) on 20 April 1889. The son of a 52-year-old customs official, Alois Schickelgruber Hitler, and his third wife, a young peasant girl, Klara Poelzl, both from the region of Lower Austria, the young Hitler was hostile to his authoritarian father, and strongly devoted to his protective and indulgent mother. There is little to suggest anything remarkable about Hitler as a boy. The school records show that he was not an outstanding student academically. His school career lasted for ten years, of which the last four were a struggle. He finally left school in September 1905 without taking any final examinations and with a poor school report that drew particular attention to his inadequate command of the German language. In Hitler's defence it should be noted that as an adolescent he was disturbed by the deaths of his younger brother Edmund (1900), his father (1903) and his beloved mother (1908). Without delving too deeply into psychological speculation about Hitler's state of mind, some biographers have suggested that these deaths (and his own survival) convinced Hitler that he was marked out by destiny for a special future.

In 1907, Hitler had moved to Vienna to seek admission to the Academy of Fine Arts. Embittered at his rejection by the Academy, he returned briefly to Linz after the death of his mother. Alone and without an occupation he left for Vienna again. Hitler later described this break with his provincial, middle-class past in dramatic terms: "With my clothes and linen packed in a valise, and with an indomitable resolution in my heart, I left for Vienna. I hoped to forestall fate, as my father had done some fifty years before. I was determined to become 'something' " (Hitler 1939: 29). He was to spend five years of "misery and woe", as he later recalled, in Vienna, leading a bohemian, vagabond existence and generally undergoing an identity crisis.

Much of the conventional views of Hitler's political and intellectual roots and antecedents will now have to be revised in the light of Brigitte Hamann's magnificent portrait of Hitler as a young man (Hamann 1999). Hamann corrects numerous misconceptions. Hitler was not, as some have claimed, of partly Jewish descent and he was never (as he himself claimed) a building worker. Moreover, Hitler did not hold his Jewish family doctor responsible for the death of his mother. In fact Hitler remained on good terms with Dr Bloch and even intervened to facilitate his emigration in 1938. Hamann also disposes of the myth that Hitler was refused entry to the Academy of Art by Jewish professors, nor was this his perception. More surprising is Hamann's detailed account of Hitler's Jewish friends and associates during his time in Vienna.

Hitler claimed he had earned a living in Vienna by hard work as a "common labourer" and only later turned himself into an artist. In fact he existed from hand to mouth on casual odd jobs, a family inheritance and hawking sketches around the city. Sleeping most mornings in a Hostel for Men in the Meldemannstrasse, he spent the evenings in cafes where he would rehearse political harangues to anyone who would care to listen. The testimonies of those who knew him during this period confirm Hitler's own account of his time in Vienna as years of great loneliness and frustration. Nevertheless these were to prove formative years in which he embraced a view of life which changed very little in the ensuing years. He later wrote: "Vienna was a hard school for me, but it taught me the most profound lessons of my life" (Hitler 1939: 32, 116).

Cosmopolitan Vienna helped shape his pathological hatred of Jews and Marxists and he began to indulge in grandiose dreams of a Greater Germany. Hitler had become a passionate German nationalist while still at school. Although the Dual Monarchy of Austria–Hungary gave the impression of stability and permanence, the irreconcilable demands of competing ethnic groups (referred to by Hitler as "bacilli") were already imposing unbearable strains on the Hapsburg Empire and the ageing Emperor Franz Joseph. Hitler despised the ramshackle and multinational Empire and fervently believed that it should be ruled by Germans without concessions to the Slavs and other subject peoples. There is an irony in the fact that Hitler's fanatical German nationalism should spring from his Austrian roots. Indeed many of Hitler's ideas can be traced to turn-of-the-century Austria–Hungary where intense nationalism had even more significance than in Germany itself.

In Vienna he began his political apprenticeship by observing the demagogic techniques of Karl Lueger, leader of the Christian Social Party and mayor of the city. Hitler admired Lueger because "he had a rare gift of insight into human nature and was very careful not to take men as something better than they were in reality" (Hitler 1939: 94). He shared Lueger's contempt for the masses and identified with his obsessive anti-Semitism with its brutal sexual connotations and concern with racial purity. In *Mein Kampf* Hitler tells us that he became a "fanatical anti-Semite" after his return to Vienna in 1908 when he encountered a "phenomenon" wearing a long kaftan and with black hair locks: "Is this a Jew? . . . is this a German?" he asked. Describing the encounter as the "greatest change I was ever to experience", Hitler steeped himself in anti-Semitic propaganda. Although we cannot be sure, he almost certainly was familiar with anti-Semitic literature in his Linz days where he had come in contact with the half-baked racial theories of the defrocked monk, Lanz von Liebenfels (and his racist periodical called *Ostara*), and the Austrian Pan-German leader, Georg von Schönerer. In fact, while Hitler continued to admire Lueger's demagogic skill, he preferred Schönerer's type of anti-Semitism as more racist. Vienna, where anti-Semitism was endemic, unquestionably fuelled his own latent anti-Semitism and transformed him into a fanatic which he remained until his death. The Jew became a total explanation for all of Hitler's hatreds, fears and desires. From now on, since he had discovered "who were the evil spirits leading our people astray", the Jew became for him the incarnation of evil and the "culprit" for all of society's ills. Thus while Hitler could sympathize with the poverty and misery of the Viennese working class, he was able to reject the class-based and anti-nationalist doctrine of social democracy on the grounds that "knowledge of the Jews is the only key whereby one may understand the inner nature and the real aims of Social Democracy" (Hitler 1939: 59, 55).

When, however, did Hitler become a paranoid anti-Semite? The 'traditional' view of Hitler's virulent anti-Semitism taking root in Vienna has been challenged by Hamann who argues that when he left Vienna for Munich in 1913 he was not the rabid anti-Semite he later became. This 'revisionist' interpretation is substantiated by Ian Kershaw in his monumental two-part biograpahy of Hitler (Kershaw 1998 and 2000). Although Hitler was certainly an anti-Semite before he arrived in Munich, Kershaw convincingly argues that the key period was the Munich period of 1918–19. Hitler's annihilatory anti-Semitism emerged from the shock of military defeat in 1918 and his extraordinary decision to enter politics (Kershaw 1998: 102–105).

Isolated and unsuccessful, Hitler moved to Munich in May 1913 at the age of 24 to avoid service in the Austrian army. However, at the outbreak of war in August 1914 Hitler enlisted in the Sixteenth Bavarian Infantry Regiment, serving as a despatch runner. He proved a courageous soldier, receiving the Iron Cross for bravery on two occasions, and was promoted to lance corporal in 1917. Twice wounded, he was badly gassed in October 1918 and spent three months recuperating in a hospital in Pomerania when the Armistice was declared. At the end of the war, amid considerable revolutionary fervour in Germany, he returned to a Munich undergoing violent political upheavals and joined the German Workers' Party (*Deutsche Arbeiterpartei* – DAP), a counter-revolutionary movement dedicated to the principles of "German national socialism", as opposed to "Jewish Marxism" or Russian Bolshevism. In the summer of 1919 he had been assigned by the *Reichswehr* (army) to spy on extremist groups in Munich and it was as a *Reichswehr* informant that he was sent to monitor the activities of the nationalist and racist German Workers' Party, led by the Munich locksmith Anton Drexler. In September 1919 he joined the DAP which comprised of 20 to 40 members and on 16 October he made his first address to the Party. With his demagogic style and strident rhetoric, Hitler discovered he possessed hidden talents for haranguing political meetings. Adolf Hitler was 30 years old and his political career had just began. He wrote in *Mein Kampf*: "Generally speaking, a man should not take part in politics before he has reached the age of thirty" (Hitler 1939: 67).

In February 1920, the DAP changed its name to the National Socialist German Workers' Party (*Nationalsozialistische Deutsche Arbeiterpartei* – NSDAP, Nazi for short) and set out its 25–point Party programme. The name at the bottom of the manifesto was not that of Hitler but of Anton Drexler. Although Hitler had only been a member of the Party for a year, the 25 points reveal the influence of his ideas. The programme contained many of the policies that became associated with the Nazis when they gained power constitutionally in 1933. Articles 1 to 3 referred to the treaties drawn up at Versailles and at St Germain (the treaty with Austria) and reflected the widespread humiliation felt by many Germans over what they believed were the "dictated" terms and conditions for peace and the failure of the newly created Weimar Republic to uphold Germany's interests as a great industrial and political power. Article 4 was explicitly racist and sought to preclude Jews from becoming citizens of Germany despite the fact that many had fought with honour for Germany during the Great War. Articles 10 and 21 referred to the duty of citizens and state to work for and ensure physical and mental fitness. These are early indications of the eugenics policy that would later be implemented by the Nazis. Interestingly, the programme anticipated a degree of state interventionism that goes beyond the staple *völkisch* ideas of other nationalist groups. War profits and some property were to be confiscated, unearned incomes abolished, trusts nationalized and department stores communalized. The old Roman law ("which serves the materialistic world order") would be replaced by a German common law. Whether these radical economic and social demands meant much to Hitler is open to doubt; more likely, they were inspired by the "socialistic" ideas of ideologues like Gottfried Feder, the Party's "economic expert". Hitler's influence can be seen in the prominence given to the myth of Aryan race supremacy and the exclusion of Jews from the *Volk* community ("national community" – *Volksgemeinschaft*). Although Hitler had presented the programme, which he had partly edited, on 24 February 1920, it had been drawn up largely without his direct help. It is doubtful that Hitler was ever wedded to the "25 points" as a philosophical blueprint; it seems more likely that he viewed it as no more than a means to an end. He had agreed to the programme simply because it reflected the radical anti-capitalism of the time and was more likely to attract disenchanted working-class and lower-middle-class support in the beerhalls and on the streets of Munich. By the late 1920s, having established himself as leader of the Party, the "socialistic" ideas of profit-sharing and nationalization had become an embarrassment and were explicitly disavowed in an attempt to woo big business and the middle classes.

Although Hitler's nationalistic ideas were scarcely distinguishable from those of a plethora of pan-German agitators, his gift for self-dramatization made an immediate impact in the beerhalls of Munich where he quickly established a reputation as a populist demagogue. The Social Democratic *Münchner Post* referred to him in August 1920 as the sharpest of all agitators "carrying out mischief in Munich". Hitler would later claim that his ideas had been firmly established before 1914. While it is true that the core of his obsessive beliefs and prejudices remained constant, in the early to mid 1920s, important modifications took place in the crystallization of his own worldview. In particular, his anti-Semitism became even more firmly linked to his antipathy towards Marxism – which in his view was its political and ideological manifestation; his own self-image underwent a process of change; and the geopolitical idea of *Lebensraum* ("living space") emerged as a central plank of Germany's future foreign policy. The experience of war, the humiliation of defeat and the revolutionary unrest in Munich all made a profound impression on Hitler and provided him with opportunities to disseminate his right-wing views. Hitler's arguments did not change appreciably – old nationalistic slogans were repeated and the Jews continued to be blamed for every political setback. Hitler even blamed the loss of the First World War on the Jews. However, after the war, the historical hatred of the Jews was increased by the credence given inside the Party to the ideas of a "Jewish world conspiracy". Alfred Rosenberg, later to became the guardian of the National Socialist *Weltanschauung* and leading theoretician of Nazi racism, had introduced Hitler to the forged *Protocols of the Elders of Zion*, according to which an international clique of Jewish conspirators were preparing to assume total domination over all nations of the world. Although the "protocols" were subsequently proved to be a Tsarist police forgery, Hitler remained convinced of their authenticity to the end of his days. Hitler's anti-Semitism, which had been an established part of his stock-in-trade, now fused with anti-Marxism into the conviction of an all-embracing Jewish–Bolshevik conspiracy. The shift appears to take place in the mid 1920s. As a result of the Russian revolution and civil war, anti-Marxism assumes an increasingly important focus for his attacks. The Jewish threat is not diminished but there is now a second factor. For Hitler the life-and-death struggle would now focus squarely on the twin evils of Judaism and Marxism. Increasingly the distinction blurred, Jews became synonymous with Bolsheviks and the "Jewish–Bolshevik" conspiracy was conflated. Hitler concluded from this that Europe was now locked in a racial struggle which only a racially cleansed Germany under his leadership could win.

By 1924 a central plank of Hitler's worldview was already established; history as a racial struggle against Judaism and its political manifestation, Marxism. Interestingly enough, Hitler's notion of the "heroic Führer-figure" and the need for *Lebensraum* in the east had not yet been fully formulated. All three would eventually fuse into an integral vision whereby the struggle to obtain more living space for Germany at the expense of Russia would lead to a historic showdown with Jewish Bolshevism and end in triumph for the German "master race" under the leadership of a heroic Führer. Before Hitler finally constructed this apocalyptic worldview there were a number of strands that still needed to fit into place. The connection between Bolshevism and Jewry continued to preoccupy him. Hitler's belief in a crude form of social Darwinism and in a racial theory of history led him to emphasize the importance of bringing the German nation to a common awareness of its ethnic and political unity. In *Mein Kampf*, for example, German *völkisch* philosophy of nineteenth-century Romanticism is contrasted with Marxism. Karl Marx ("a Jew") and international Marxism are attacked precisely for their failure to recognize the value of race and "for a denial of the *differences* [my italics] between races". According to Hitler the "bourgeois world" had been infected by these "poisons", while "Marxism itself systematically plans to hand the world over to the Jews". By contrast, the *völkisch* philosophy embraced by National Socialism "finds the importance of mankind in its basic elements". Such a belief, claimed Hitler, promotes "the victory of the better and the stronger, and demand[s] the subordination of the inferior and weaker in accordance with the eternal will that dominates the universe" (Hitler 1939: 347–9).

The antecedents of these racist beliefs can be traced to the works of writers like Gobineau and, more importantly, Houston Stewart Chamberlain who prophesied a German *Herrenvolk* (Master Race). Hitler never really bothered to formulate a coherent picture of what he meant by "race"; instead he drew upon these ideas and argued that the purest and most creative contemporary race was the "Aryan", a race whose inward qualities were intrinsically linked to its external appearance. Although he never precisely defined the term, the notion of a superior Germanic people ("Aryans") offered a pseudo-scientific explanation for the Germanic myth of racial purity as the antithesis of "corruptible alien elements". These elements he identified as Judaism and Marxism. Significantly, Hitler always referred to Jews as a biologically determined race, not as a religion. According to this "theory" Jews were the historical enemy of Aryans because they had no homeland (what would Hitler have made of Israel?), they were lazy, materialistic, self-seeking and incapable of making sacrifices for the greater communal good. Hitler went even further: "If the Jews were alone in the world, they would stifle in dirt and offal . . . or try to exterminate one another in a hate-filled struggle". Moreover, because Jews were rootless they attempted to subvert "real" nations and became parasitical upon them. Hitler claimed that Russia had been destroyed by Jews:

By abandoning Russia to Bolshevism, Fate robbed the Russian nation of that educated class which previously brought about and guaranteed its existence as a State . . . Impossible as it is for the Russian by himself to shake off the yoke of the Jew by his own resources, it is equally impossible for the Jew to maintain the mighty empire for ever. He himself is not an element of organisation but a ferment of decomposition. The giant Empire in the east is ripe for collapse. And the end of Jewish rule in Russia will also be the end of Russia as a state (Hitler 1939: 742).

To the end of his days, Hitler remained convinced that Jewish Bolshevism and Western culture could not co-exist. The only possible outcome was the destruction of one of these forces. For Hitler, the destruction of Marxism and the destruction of the Jews were identical goals – and this was to be the historic task of a "Germanic state of the German nation".

Hitler's belief in the authenticity of the *Protocols of the Elders of Zion* and the success of "Jewish Bolshevism" in Russia had implications for his thinking on German foreign policy. Hitler's racial philosophy led him to demand *Lebensraum* for Germans and his adherence to social Darwinism convinced him that war was a "natural" part of history and the ultimate test of a nation's spiritual and moral fibre. But where would this living space be found? Hitler rejected the "scramble" for colonial acquisitions taken by the Kaiser prior to 1914, arguing that such a policy had antagonized England and led to an unnecessary war. He fixed his gaze instead on eastern Europe and Russia in particular. A war with Soviet Russia, Hitler concluded, would prove attractive to the nations of western Europe in its struggle against the insidious threat of Bolshevism. It would also prove once and for all the superiority of the Aryan peoples over Jewish and Slav influence. A German victory would crush international Marxism and international finance (the "Jewish–Bolshevik conspiracy") and allow Germans to re-settle in the east.

> We national Socialists will stop the endless German drive to the south and west and turn our gaze towards the land in the East. At long last we break off the colonial and commercial policy of the pre-War period and shift to the soil policy of the future. And when we speak of soil in Europe today, we think primarily of Russia and her vassal border states. To the East, and only to the East, must we divert our excess births (Hitler 1939: 742).

In the summer of 1928, Hitler dictated the text of his *Zweites Buch* (*Second book*, or *Secret book*) which dealt far more than *Mein Kampf* with his economic and, by extension, his foreign policy thinking. While John Toland (Toland 1976: 230–32) notoriously exaggerates the significance of the *Second Book* (that was left unpublished in Hitler's own lifetime), Kershaw contends, rightly, in my opinion, that the work 'offers nothing new' (Kershaw 1998: 291). Hitler invariably spoke of *Raumnot* (shortage of territory) rather than *Lebensraum* (living space). His thinking, however, remained consistent: German economic expansion was hindered by a "shortage of space" and space could only be attained by the use of force. Hitler wrote that politics is the 'art of carrying out a people's struggle for its earthly existence' whereas foreign policy is the art of 'safeguarding ... living space, in quantity and quality, for a people' (Hitler 1961: 24). He argued that a people are conditioned by laws of nature which drive them to acquire food and reproduce. Given that space is finite then competition for scarce territory will inevitably result in conflict: 'Thus the bread of freedom grows from the hardships of war. The sword was the pathbreaker for the plough' (Hitler, 1961, 15).

Hitler's deepening engagement with foreign policy and *Raumfragen* (territorial issues) coincided with his growing interest in the leitmotiv of personality and his ideas of heroic leadership for Germany. Hitler argued that the state was the means of securing a victory over "Jewish Bolshevism", but the state required the inspiration and guidance of a heroic leader-figure. It was while he was in prison in Landsberg in 1924 for high treason, after the abortive Munich *Putsch*, that Hitler came to see himself as the future "great leader". Prior to his imprisonment he had talked about messianic leadership but had seen himself merely as the "drummer" facilitating the way. As early as 1922, no doubt influenced by the example of Mussolini in Italy, Hitler began to stress the centrality of a Führer-figure as an integrating mechanism of the Nazi movement. Hitler had just emerged victorious from a power struggle of his own with his powers greatly enhanced. By 1921 it was clear that the Party was rapidly distancing itself from the original conception of Anton Drexler and members of the Party committee. Hitler's attempts to turn the Party into a mass movement, his propaganda methods and his personal antipathy towards the "Drexler wing" came to a head in July 1921 when Drexler tried to recapture the direction of the Party citing Hitler's "lust for power and personal ambition" and his unwillingness to merge with other rival *völkisch* groups. Refusing to make concessions, Hitler resigned on 11 July demanding, as preconditions for his return, the retirement of the committee and dictatorial powers for himself. At extraordinary meetings of 26 and 29 July Hitler was elected President with unlimited powers forcing poor Anton Drexler into the political wilderness with the valedictory title of Honorary President. A few days later on 3 August, the foundations of the SA (*Sturmabteilung* – stormtroopers), the Party's paramilitary wing, were formed. (Hitler would later demand similar unlimited powers, eventually combining the roles of head of state, head of government, head of party and Supreme Commander in the unique title of Führer of the German People.)

Following his takeover of the Party leadership, the roots of the personality cult around Hitler became more noticeable and increasingly his followers referred to him as "our Führer". Indeed, at one meeting in Munich in 1922, Hermann Esser, one of the Party's leading figures, proclaimed Hitler to be Germany's Mussolini. The content of Hitler's speeches at this time also suggest that a discernible shift was taking place in Hitler's own concept of heroic leadership and he was beginning to see himself as the "Führer".

Having established his authority in the Party and reshaped its leadership structure, Hitler now decided to challenge the resolve of the Weimar Republic by mounting a *Putsch* in the Nazi stronghold of Bavaria. No doubt influenced by Mussolini's successful march on Rome in October 1922, Hitler decided to act. Taking advantage of Germany's hyper-inflation, the French and Belgian occupation of the Ruhr and government instability, Hitler together with disaffected war hero General Ludendorff and local nationalist groups sought to overthrow the Bavarian government in Munich and then march on "red" Berlin. On the evening of 8 November 1923 Hitler mobilized units of the SA and burst into a public meeting at the Bürgerbräu-Keller in Munich where the Bavarian state government under Gustav von Kahr was deciding whether or not to establish a separatist rightwing regime independent from alleged socialist influence in Berlin. Brandishing a gun, Hitler declared that he was forming a new provisional government: "I am going to fulfil the vow I made five years ago when I was a blind cripple in the military hospital; to know neither rest nor peace until the November criminals had been overthrown, until on the ruins of the wretched Germany of today there should have arisen once more a Germany of power and greatness, of freedom and splendour". The following morning Hitler and Ludendorff marched through Munich at the head of 3,000 men, only to be halted by police fire which left 16 Nazis and three police dead and brought the attempted *Putsch* (or more accurately, demonstration) to a humiliating and ignominious end.

Hitler's plans had badly misfired. Hitler was arrested and tried in an old Munich infantry school on 26 February 1924. The trial lasted for 24 days and by the end of it Hitler had emerged as a national figure. He was accused of high treason and sentenced to only five years' imprisonment in Landsberg; the leniency of the minimum sentence reflected the right-wing nationalist sympathies of the judiciary. Hitler, who was not even a German citizen, had gained in confidence throughout the proceedings and at the end of the trial skilfully turned the tables on his accusers with an emotional propaganda speech which ended with the prophecy: "Pronounce us guilty a thousand times over: the goddess of the eternal court of history will smile and tear to pieces the State Prosecutor's submission and the sentence of this court. For she acquits us." Despite the severity of the crime, Hitler was released after only nine months, during which time he dictated the first volume of *Mein Kampf* to his loyal followers, Rudolf Hess and Emil Maurice. Hitler was permitted to remain in Germany. He was banned from speaking in Bavaria and kept his head down during the year after his release, concentrating on writing the second volume of *Mein Kampf*. By assuming full responsibility for the attempted overthrow of the Republic and refusing to make concessions to the authorities, Hitler transformed the débâcle of the failed *Putsch* into a personal triumph.

The failure of the Munich *Putsch* and his period of imprisonment elevated Hitler from an obscure provincial right-wing politician into a national figure, a symbol of implacable opposition to the Republic and the new figurehead of the *völkisch* movement. Hitler's performance at his "show trial" demonstrated once again his considerable gift as a speaker (something he discovered for the first time in February 1920 when addressing a crowd of over 2,000 in Munich). Hitler understood the art of public speaking, of silence, of pauses, of inducing, inciting and inflaming passion. Referring to this aspect of Hitler's personality many years later, Albert Speer confessed: "I became committed [to Hitler] when I first heard him speak ... I was enthusiastic, elated; I felt that he could save Germany, give us back faith in ourselves ... I am ashamed of it now, but at the time, I found him deeply exciting" (Sereny 1995: 89, 98).

The following nine months in Landsberg provided Hitler with the opportunity to lecture his fellow Nazi inmates (literally a captive audience) on his ideas. The result was *Mein Kampf*. The significance of *Mein Kampf* is often overlooked by historians. *Mein Kampf* is turgid, it is repetitious and it is irrational and misleading. However, such stylistic and critical analysis, focusing on unquestioned deficiencies, overlooks other important propaganda aspects of the work. Hitler was not an intellectual, and in fact never claimed to be one. As

we have already seen, he retained a widespread suspicion of intellectuals and formal learning. But Hitler always placed great faith in
the spoken word, more so than the written word. "False ideas and
ignorance may be set aside by means of instruction, but emotional
resistance never can. Nothing but an appeal to hidden forces will be
effective here. And that appeal can scarcely be made by any writer.
Only the orator can hope to make it" (Hitler 1939: 392). This is not
surprising given Hitler's skill as an orator. Written while Hitler was
incarcerated in Landsberg prison and thus denied an audience, *Mein
Kampf* was intended to render the spoken word. Unable to address
his audience in person, Hitler dictated his ideas instead. The text of
Mein Kampf is thus a piece of political demagogy in prose. Hitler did
not write *Mein Kampf*, he spoke it! Much of the book (this "spoken
book") is simply an outpouring of Hitler's half-baked ideas and
prejudices and a substitute for personally addressing party meetings.
It was "written" as a work of political propaganda. The translation
into English is a considerable improvement on the German original.

The extent to which *Mein Kampf* constituted a blueprint which the
Party systematically implemented when it came to power in 1933
remains a source of intense historiographical debate. A.J.P. Taylor
dismissed it as mere daydreams, the expression of "dogmas which
echo the conversation of any Austrian café or German beer house"
(Taylor 1961: 69). James Joll, on the other hand, argued that "such
views underestimated both Hitler and his book". For Joll, *Mein
Kampf* contains "all of Hitler's beliefs, most of his programme and
much of his character" (Joll 1973: 332). It is true that much of what
Hitler expressed in *Mein Kampf* was implemented in the Third Reich
(dismantling of the terms of the Versailles Treaty, destruction of
parliamentary democracy, unleashing a world war, the persecution
and genocide of Jews). This has underpinned the "intentionalist"
argument that Hitler can be seen as *the* "programmatist" carrying out
systematically his ideological objectives. In recent years there has
been a move away from this "Hitlerist" approach to stress more
the "structural" constraints on policy and the arbitrary nature of
decision-making during the Third Reich. "Structuralists" point to
Hitler's unwillingness or inability to take tough decisions that might
undermine his popularity. In arbitrating between the two schools of
thought, Ian Kershaw has suggested that "Hitler's ideology has been
seen less as a 'programme' consistently implemented than as a loose

framework for action which only gradually stumbled into the shape of realisable objectives" (Kershaw 1991: 7). Bearing in mind that Hitler had only just embarked upon a political career and remained largely peripheral to mainstream politics, it is doubtful that in 1924 he was in a position realistically to set out a blueprint for a specific programme in *Mein Kampf*. Written while its author was imprisoned and unable to speak to his followers, *Mein Kampf* is a "stream of consciousness" that reflected Hitler's prejudices at a time when he (and his party) were far removed from the centre stage of Weimar politics. In many respects it is an attempt to extend his obsessive hatred of Jews into a full-scale ideology. Together with the *Second book* it is the most revealing indictment of his early racist and expansionist views that exists. *Mein Kampf*, as his biographer Joachim Fest has perceptively stated, "conveys a remarkably faithful portrait of its author, who in his constant fear of being unmasked actually unmasks himself" (Fest 1974: 304).

In the light of policies that were later implemented, *Mein Kampf* cannot be ignored or underestimated – or simply dismissed as the product of a deranged mind. Kershaw's notion of a "framework for action" (or more accurately, Martin Broszat, who was the first to refer to "guidelines for action" in 1970) strikes a balanced judgement. *Mein Kampf* was compulsory reading for all Nazi followers and was offered up in millions of copies as official reading matter. It is inconceivable that rank-and-file bureaucrats and local functionaries, charged with implementing government policy during the Third Reich, believed that they were carrying out anything other than the wishes of their Führer. Until the edifice of the Third Reich began to crumble, *Mein Kampf* remained an "official" source of reference and legitimized much of Nazi practice. This debate will be explored in greater detail in Chapters 4 and 5.

Following the fiasco of the Beer Hall *Putsch*, the Nazi Party had been banned and Rosenberg, Hitler's choice as temporary leader, was incapable of asserting his authority. It suited Hitler for the Party to remain weak and divided during his detention and confirmed the indispensability of his leadership – which is why Hitler had chosen Rosenberg in the first place. On his release Hitler had the task of re-establishing his authority and the direction of the movement. He concluded that the road to power lay through the legal subversion of the Weimar Constitution, the building of a mass movement and the combination of parliamentary strength with extra-parliamentary violence and intimidation. The ban on the Nazi Party and its paper (*Völkischer Beobachter*) was lifted in January 1925 and on 26 February the NSDAP was officially re-founded ("A New Beginning") with Hitler as its first member. The Bavarian authorities did, however, ban Hitler from speaking in public in March 1925 (until March 1927), although he was permitted to speak to closed Party gatherings. Hitler's performance at his trial, his incarceration and the publication of *Mein Kampf* helped both to sustain the personality cult developing around Hitler and establish him as the "programmatist" of the Nazi movement. Hitler by now was possessed by delusions of grandeur. Convinced that he was *the* Leader, with a heroic mission, he could no longer be constrained from comparing himself to historical figures such as Frederick the Great. In a speech he made in May 1926, ostensibly on Bismarck, but clearly alluding to himself, he informed his audience that "It was necessary to implant the national idea within the masses ... and only a *giant* [my italics] could complete this task". Hitler's audiences would have recognized the contemporary significance of such references. Convinced that he was Germany's political messiah, his supporters unashamedly referred to Hitler as a prophet. A number have talked about how they had been "spellbound" by the power of Hitler's personality. After reading *Mein Kampf*, Joseph Goebbels, later the Party's propaganda chief, wrote "Who is this man? half plebeian, half God! Truly Christ, or only St John?" For the growing number of "disciples" gathering around Hitler at this time – referred to as the "charismatic community" – Hitler was more than just a politician offering political and economic solutions, he was a messianic leader embodying the salvation of Germany. Interestingly enough, he was also a stateless person. Some three months after his release from Landsberg in April 1925, Hitler applied successfully to the authorities in his native Linz for release from Austrian citizenship. From 1925 until he was appointed a state councillor in February 1932 (when he became a German citizen having sworn an oath of loyalty to the constitution of the German Reich and Länder), he remained a stateless person.

With the re-establishment of the Party in February 1925, Hitler's position and status was greatly enhanced. Potential rivals such as the North German *völkisch* leaders, Graefe and Reventlow, had broken away, disaffected, and drifted into other parties. The most serious challenge to his authority, however, came at the Party meeting in Bamberg in February 1926. In a five-hour speech Hitler headed off an attempt by the North German wing of the Party under Gregor Strasser (the second most powerful man in the Party) to rewrite the Party programme along more "socialist" lines. By stressing his commitment to the 1920 programme and demanding loyalty to the Führer, Hitler outmanoeuvred his rivals and preserved the unity of the Party. Hitler's triumph was compounded by the capture of Goebbels, hitherto one of Strasser's strongest supporters. Writing in his diary in April 1926, Goebbels referred to Hitler as a "genius" and added "Adolf Hitler, I love you" (quoted in Heiber 1960: 74). At the first Party Congress to be held since the *Putsch* in July, the charismatic nature of Hitler's leadership and his claim to absolute authority was unanimously confirmed in a demonstration of Party unity. Commenting on the significance of these events, Ian Kershaw has written: "The way to the fully fledged 'Führer Party' was paved" (Kershaw 1991: 45).

The crisis was over. Having eliminated rivals from within the movement and reshaped its organizational structure in his own image Hitler imposed his unimpeachable authority over the movement. When Otto Strasser precipitated a similar challenge in 1930, Hitler's position and authority were unquestioned and Strasser was peremptorily dismissed from the Party. Finally, in December 1932, Gregor Strasser resigned following a fundamental split over the primacy of the Party's original ideas set against unconditional faith in the Führer. On this occasion, Strasser's resignation did not lead to a split in the Party – or indeed to any form of factionalism. Hitler retained the loyalty of the movement. Henceforth, Hitler devoted much of his energy to reinvigorating Party cells and generally strengthening the Party nationally. Hitler concentrated on the short-term goal of gaining power on a "catch-all" platform of national resurgence. To achieve this he decided to dismantle the organizational structure of the Party that his great rival Strasser had erected and concentrate on seducing the electorate by means of propaganda. This required cynically disregarding many of the principles of the Party's 1920 programme – except those that constituted a means to power.

The period between the re-founding of the NSDAP in February 1925 and the Reichstag elections of July 1932 when the Nazis emerged as the largest political party in Germany marks a sea-change in their fortunes. Nevertheless it is important to remind ourselves just how insignificant Hitler and the NSDAP were to the centre stage of Weimar politics in the period leading up to their electoral breakthrough. In the 1928 elections the Nazis polled only 2.6 per cent of the vote (12 seats). Significant, however, was the growing strength of their activist base which increased to over 100,000 members. The onset of the Depression with its devastating effects on the German middle and working classes helped win support. But equally, much of the success must be attributed to the creation of the "Führer-myth" and the quasi-religious identification of the movement with its leader, Adolf Hitler. Nazi propaganda that depicted Hitler as an uncompromising opponent of the Weimar Republic had the effect of setting Hitler apart from other politicians tainted by their association with the Weimar system which had now become synonymous with political humiliation and economic failure. Symbolic of the intensification of the "cult of leader" was the compulsory "Heil Hitler" greeting for all Party members. The umbilical bond within this "charismatic community" became so closely identified with the absolute authority of its leader that when Germans voted in elections in the 1930s the ballot card referred not to the NSDAP but to the "Hitler movement" (*Hitlerbewegung*).

By the time Hitler was appointed Chancellor in 1933, the edifice of his "worldview" was in place. It had been constructed as a result of a series of formative and overlapping experiences. Hitler had successfully imposed on his Party his racist vision and the need to remove Jews from Germany and for territorial expansion in the east for a German *Herrenvolk* (master race). Although he continued notionally to reaffirm his commitment to the radical Nazi programme of 1920, in practice he had steered clear of too many pronouncements on economic policy – conscious of the need to attract big business and the support of certain German elites. In this sense he was no revolutionary in the Lenin mould, rather an intuitive opportunist determined to gain power first in order to impose his "utopian visions". Writing about Hitler in the period preceding the takeover of the state, Alan Bullock has referred to a disturbing combination of ambition, energy and indolence. This is true and reflects the complexity and paradoxical nature of Hitler's personality and character. When the Nazis gained power, Hitler was placed in a position to implement his ideas. The electorate could have been left in little doubt as to what they could expect. Hitler had set out his views unambiguously to all those prepared to listen.

CHAPTER TWO

Gaining power

The 1928 elections brought to power the so-called "Grand Coalition" consisting of the Social Democratic Party (SPD) together with a number of middle-class parties. Within two years this much heralded coalition, which had been elected with such high expectations, had collapsed and Hitler would emerge out of a labyrinth of power struggles to form a government. As Dick Geary has reminded us, the massive transformation in the fortunes of the NSDAP in such a short period of time suggests that the Nazis' success was not simply a consequence of the Party's propaganda and Hitler's charisma, "but also depended upon the climate within which Weimar politicians operated" (Geary 1993: 12). In January 1933, von Schleicher's government, which had attempted to conciliate both Centre and Leftist interests within the Weimar system, was unable to secure a majority in the Reichstag and resigned. On 30 January, the President, Field Marshal Hindenburg, accepted a cabinet with Hitler as Chancellor, von Papen (the former Chancellor and leader of the Catholic Centre Party) as Vice-Chancellor and nationalists including Nazis in other posts. Hitler did not owe his appointment as Chancellor to a victory at a national election. Instead, in Alan Bullock's phrase, he was "jobbed into office by a backstairs intrigue".

Nevertheless, despite the political machinations that took place within high politics prior to his appointment, Hitler became Chancellor constitutionally. The suggestion that Hitler and his party somehow "seized" power is rather misleading. The Nazis themselves are largely responsible for perpetuating this myth by continuing to refer to a *Kampfzeit* (period of struggle) and to their *Machtergreifung* (seizure of power). Having gained power the Nazis used the Reichstag fire of 27 February 1933 as a pretext for suspending civil liberties (Reichstag Fire Decree) and conducting an election campaign (which had already begun) in circumstances highly favourable to themselves. In the elections of 5 March the NSDAP made further gains, winning 288 seats, but failed to secure an overall majority, taking only 43.9 per cent of the vote.

In this chapter I want to look at the means employed by the Nazis that led to their electoral success and particularly to reappraise the view that Hitler somehow "conquered the masses" and that propaganda alone had "brainwashed" the German people into electing him. Merely to talk in terms of the "conquest of the masses" implies the manipulation or seduction of millions into voting for a leader and a party in apparent disregard for their own best interests, the assumption being that these voters, who might otherwise have resisted Nazism, were "mesmerized" by a well-functioning propaganda machine. The danger of such an approach is that it concentrates on the "techniques of persuasion" at the expense of a detached analysis of the programme put forward by Hitler and the NSDAP to solve fundamental economic and social problems. Such an approach leads to the inevitable conclusion that to vote for the Nazi manifesto was an "irrational" act. This does not solve the question of why millions of Germans acted in such an apparently irrational way. It seems clear that many groups, rather than being "seduced" by Nazi propaganda, perceived voting for Hitler and the NSDAP as being in their own interests and that Nazi propaganda served to reinforce such beliefs. Similarly, other groups remained stubbornly resistant to the Nazi message, and no amount of skilful propaganda could persuade them otherwise. To over-emphasize the importance of propaganda would be to diminish the failings of the Weimar *system* to solve prevailing economic and social problems and for political opponents of the NSDAP to provide viable alternatives. If, as seems likely, many Germans reluctantly voted for the Nazi Party because there seemed to be little credible alternative, then that is not necessarily the outcome of propaganda alone, but the failure of the Weimar system. It is therefore imperative to re-examine the manner in which propaganda disseminated the Nazi programme and to distinguish between supporters and opponents of the NSDAP and those who remained indifferent.

Electoral success

Before discussing who voted for Hitler and why, it might be useful to begin with a brief outline of the political performance of the Nazi Party during the final years of the Weimar Republic in order to set their political achievement in some sort of context. In 1928, a mere 810,127 electors voted for the NSDAP; four years later, in July 1932, this figure had increased to a staggering 13,765,781. Support for the Nazis in national elections between May 1928 and September 1930 rose from 810,127 (2.6 per cent of the total) to 6,379,672 votes (18.3 per cent) – an eightfold increase! By July 1932 the NSDAP was the largest party in the Reichstag with 37.3 per cent of the total vote and 230 seats in the Reichstag, almost a hundred more than their nearest rivals the Social Democrats (SPD). In the elections of November 1932 the Nazis suffered a minor setback when their percentage of the vote was reduced to 33.1 per cent (196 seats). Nevertheless, the combined electoral successes of 1932 helped pave the way for Hitler's assumption of the Chancellorship in January 1933. As economic and social conditions deteriorated between 1928 and 1930, membership of the NSDAP also continued to grow although not to the same extent as the explosion of the Nazi vote. In October 1928 Nazi Party membership had reached 100,000; in September 1930, 300,000; and by the end of 1931, membership exceeded 800,000. One can see therefore that the most rapid increase in membership occurred after the election victories of 1930 and was thus the result not the cause of the Party's electoral breakthrough.

Hitler's thoughts on propaganda

The appeal of National Socialism is understandably one of the most closely studied issues in European history. Historians have been concerned to explain why millions of Germans voted for the Nazi Party (NSDAP) in free elections. Their success has been attributed in large measure to successful manipulation by a propaganda machine. The skilful exploitation of propaganda techniques has been cited by historians of widely different political persuasions and approaches as having played a crucial role in mobilizing support for the Nazis. In this context, attention has by and large been focused on the dynamics of the Nazi Party, its parades, its symbols, the uniforms and banners, the bands, the marching columns of the SA, etc., which "captured the imagination" of the masses. In the light of such consensus, it would appear that one of the most important factors contributing to the Nazis' rise to power was the cumulative effect of their propaganda; certainly the Nazis themselves were convinced of its effectiveness. In *Mein Kampf*, Hitler devoted two chapters to the study and practice of propaganda. In 1925, when *Mein Kampf* was first published, Hitler's thoughts on war propaganda were largely a reflection of the prevailing nationalist claims that Allied propaganda was responsible for the collapse of the German Empire in 1918. Convinced of the essential role of propaganda for any movement set on obtaining power, Hitler saw propaganda as a vehicle of political salesmanship in a mass market; he argued that the consumers of propaganda were the masses and not the intellectuals. In answer to his own question, "to whom should propaganda be addressed – to the scientifically trained intelligentsia or to the less educated masses?", he answered emphatically, "it must be addressed always and exclusively to the masses". Hitler made no attempt to hide his contempt for the masses and what he would do in power. According to Hitler, they were malleable and corrupt, "overwhelmingly feminine by nature and attitude", and as such their sentiment was not complicated, "but very simple and consistent". In other words, they were influenced not by their brains but by their emotions. In *Mein Kampf*, where Hitler laid down the broad lines along which Nazi propaganda was to operate, he assessed his audience as follows:

> The receptivity of the great masses is very limited, their intelligence is small, but their power of forgetting is enormous. In consequence, all effective propaganda must be limited to a very few points and must harp on these in slogans until the last member of the public understands what you want him to understand by your slogan (Hitler 1939: 165).

The function of propaganda, Hitler argued, was "to see that an idea wins supporters ... it tries to force a doctrine on the whole people". To achieve this, propaganda was to bring the masses' attention to certain facts, processes, necessities, etc., "whose significance is thus for the first time placed within their field of vision". Accordingly, propaganda for the masses had to be simple, it had to concentrate on as few points as possible which then had to be repeated many times, concentrating on such emotional elements as love and hatred. "Persistence is the first and most important requirement for success." Through the continuity and sustained uniformity of its application, propaganda, Hitler concluded, would lead to results "that are almost beyond our understanding". Therefore, unlike the Bolsheviks, Hitler did not make a distinction between agitation and propaganda. In Soviet Russia agitation was concerned with influencing the masses through ideas and slogans, while propaganda served to spread the Communist ideology of Marxist-Leninism. The distinction dates back to Plekhanov's famous definition, written in 1892: "A propagandist presents *many* ideas to one or a few persons; an agitator presents *only one* or *a few* ideas, but presents them to a *whole* mass of people." Hitler, on the other hand, did not regard propaganda as merely an instrument for reaching the party elite, but rather as a means for the persuasion and indoctrination of all Germans.

Hitler's theories on propaganda were first put into practice in 1925 in the NSDAP newspaper, the *Völkischer Beobachter* (*People's Observer*). The Nazis had bought the newspaper in 1920 when it had a small circulation in and around the Munich area, but following the failure of the *Putsch* in 1923, the newspaper had disappeared from newspaper stands until 26 February 1925 – the official date of the "re-establishment" of the Party. Within two months of its re-launch it had become a daily newspaper and its circulation began to rise until in 1929 it had reached a figure of 26,715. Unlike the long, detailed articles and academic discussion of economic and social problems which characterized the political presses of the Weimar Republic, the *Völkischer Beobachter* went in for short, punchy hyperboles on typical National Socialist themes – the evil of Jewry and Bolshevism, the humiliation of the Versailles Treaty, the weakness of Weimar parliamentarianism, all of which were contrasted with Nazi patriotic slogans such as "Ein Volk, Ein Reich, Ein Führer" ("One People, One Nation, One Leader") – later to be used to great effect in the 1938 campaign for an *Anschluss* (union) with Austria (see Chapter 4). Convinced more than ever that propaganda was a powerful weapon in the hands of an expert, Hitler appointed Joseph Goebbels Head of Party Propaganda in April 1930 with the mission to centralize the Party's propaganda machinery and present the Nazis' remorseless march to triumph under the leadership of the Führer. Goebbels had launched *Der Angriff* (*The Attack*), the other major Nazi newspaper, in 1927 with the challenging motto "For the Oppressed! Against the Exploiters!" on the front page. Under Goebbels' direction the Party showed an increasing opportunism for learning and adapting new propaganda techniques. A recurring slogan was "Deutschland erwache, Juda verrecke!" ("Germany awake, Jewry be dammed!"). The essentially negative anti-parliamentarianism and anti-Semitism of National Socialist propaganda allowed Goebbels to use *Der Angriff* as a vehicle for the dissemination of one of the most important positive themes in Nazi propaganda, namely the projection of the "Führer-myth", which depicted Hitler as both charismatic superman and a man of the people.

Who voted for the Nazis – and why?

As we have already seen, the NSDAP's electoral breakthrough occurred between 1928 and 1930. How can one explain this dramatic increase in the Nazi vote and what role did propaganda play in securing this electoral success?

Recent research into Nazi voting patterns suggests that after 1928 the NSDAP performed best in the predominantly Protestant and rural districts of the North German plain, whereas the large cities and urban connurbations, together with predominantly Catholic rural areas in the west and south, proved more resistant to the Nazi appeal. These are, of course, broad generalizations and it is quite clear that manual workers in the cities, as well as Catholics, were prepared to vote for the NSDAP as well. The conclusion that can be drawn from electoral figures about social composition show that despite the disproportionate number of Protestant, rural and middle-class sup-porters, the NSDAP could justifiably claim to represent a wider range of economic and social groups than any other political party. Individuals and groups were prepared to desert traditional allegiances (mainly Protestant middle-class parties) and vote for the Nazis for different reasons. Most historians would agree, however, that the *Hitlerbewegung* (Hitler movement) successfully integrated the German middle class. First, it won support from the "old middle class" of small retailers, self-employed artisans, peasant farmers, pensioners and those on fixed incomes. Secondly it also appealed to the "new middle class" of white-collar, non manual employees. Under the Second Reich both of these groups had shared a sense of their own identity that made them the backbone of the nation. They were known collectively as the *Mittelstand*, the healthy core in the middle of German society. With the collapse of the German Empire in 1918, the values and assumptions that had shaped and buttressed the *Mittelstand* were suddenly removed. The Weimar Republic represented an acute threat to their status. Some looked to the Nazis as the saviour of old-style capitalism that would restore the old status quo. For such groups, the Nazis represented a "reactionary" force restoring former status and values. Others, particularly among younger white-collar workers, saw National Socialism as a "revolutionary" movement bent on destroying archaic social hierarchies and replacing them with a new social order. The secret of their success was this "dual" appeal.

As the economic crisis deepened and class tension increased, the various sections of the *Mittelstand* came together within the Nazi movement. The *Hitlerbewegung* was the "mobilization of disaffection" and as such far more successful than the traditional political parties who had become discredited through their association with the Republic and its failure to redress genuine or imagined grievances. There can be little doubt that under Goebbels' direction, the NSDAP exploited these grievances for the purposes of propaganda. By means of an efficient propaganda apparatus that Goebbels had been building up since 1930, the Party was in a strong position to make a highly effective reponse to the growing sense of crisis and through its propaganda to appeal to both the interests and the ideals of the *Mittelstand*. Indeed, some historians have suggested that towards the end of 1927 with the fall in agricultural prices, and following its failure in the 1928 Reichstag elections, there was a significant reorientation in the Party's propaganda away from the industrial working class in the urban conurbations towards a series of campaigns aimed at the *Mittelstand* in the rural areas. More recently there have been attempts to look again at Nazi efforts to mobilize the alienated urban proletariat. By the early part of 1932 Goebbels was confident enough to write: "The election campaign is ready in principle. We now only need to press the button in order to set the machine into action."

With unemployment exceeding six million and the Weimar Republic sinking into its death throes, the 1932 elections were fought in a growing atmosphere of political violence and disorder. By January 1933, Hitler had obtained the support of the army and sections of industry, and on 30 January he was constitutionally appointed Chancellor by President Hindenburg. The Nazis' political success in opposition has frequently been attributed to Goebbels' manipulatory talents. There can be little doubt that Nazi propaganda was quick to seize its opportunity and that it was firmly based on the principles outlined by Hitler in *Mein Kampf*. It carried through with a ruthless consistency a campaign of propaganda which appealed directly to the emotions rather than to the intellect, and was reinforced at all levels by terror and violence. But propaganda alone cannot change social and political conditions; it acts in conjunction with other factors, like organization. As Dick Geary has pointed out, the Nazi message reached "parts of Germany other parties did not reach" (Geary 1993: 29).

While the Nazis' propaganda machine was important in helping achieve this electoral victory, the NSDAP was in the fortunate political position, unlike almost every other party in the Weimar Republic, of appealing to different groups for different reasons. Hitler and his party recognized not simply the importance of propaganda, but more importantly the need to adapt its propaganda to these different groups. National Socialist propaganda did not destroy Weimar democracy, although it did undermine it. What distinguished the Hitler Movement from other parties in opposition was its ability to combine the themes of traditional German nationalism with Nazi ideological motifs. By unifying German patriotism with Nazi ideology Hitler forged a compelling weapon against what he referred to as the "immorality of Weimar rationalism" and its associations for many (including non-Nazis) with cultural decadence and racial impurity. To this end, Hitler alone was perceived by many groups to represent certain ideas that appeared to transcend Weimar politics. This not only gave Hitler and the Nazis a wider appeal, but it also set them apart from other political parties.

Key themes exploited by Nazi propaganda

There can be little doubt that the two most important ideas that distinguished the Nazis from other parties and allowed Nazi

propaganda to mobilize widespread grievances were the notion of
Volksgemeinschaft (community of the people) based on the principle
laid down in the party programme of 1920 "*Gemeinnutz geht vor
Eigennutz*" ("Common good before the good of the individual") and
the myth of the "charismatic Führer". The "community of the people"
was to replace the "divisive" party system and the class barriers of the
Weimar Republic and in effect offer the prospect of national unity
without either a bloody revolution or the need to offer too many
concessions to the working class. The other element which appears to
have been genuinely effective and unique was the projection of Hitler
as a charismatic leader. The Führer cult had become synonymous with
the NSDAP and it is significant that the Party referred to itself on the
ballot papers as the "Hitler Movement". From 1930 onward, its
panache in staging political rallies, where Hitler could project his
leadership and the faithful could give the impression of being a
dynamic movement, far exceeded that of other parties. The carefully
constructed mass rallies with their marches, banners and flags, when
combined with Hitler's histrionic speeches, provided Goebbels with
the opportunity to synthesize the twin concepts of *Volksgemeinschaft*
and the Führer cult in one political experience.

The ritual of the mass meeting was an important element in the
projection of the Führer cult. Uniforms, bands, flags, and symbols
were all part of Goebbels' propaganda machine to increase the impact
of Hitler's strong words with strong deeds. This is the fundamental
rationale behind the constant display of Nazi symbols in posters and
in films like *Triumph of the Will* (*Triumph des Willens*, 1935) and the
weekly German newsreels (*Deutsche Wochenschauen*). Leni Riefen-
stahl's *Triumph of the Will*, the documentary film commissioned by
Hitler of the 1934 *Reichsparteitag*, opens with a slow fade-up of the
German eagle and the title, with the caption "Twenty years after the
outbreak of the First World War, sixteen years after the beginning of
Germany's time of trial, nineteen months after the beginning of the
rebirth of Germany, Adolf Hitler flew to Nuremberg to muster his
faithful followers ...". In projecting the image of the strong leader to
an audience that had come to associate the Weimar Republic and the
Treaty of Versailles with national ignominy, *Triumph des Willens*
portrayed Hitler as a statesman of genius who had single-handedly
rebuilt the nation and staunchly defended Germany's territorial rights
over the hegemony imposed by foreigners. (This theme is taken up in

Chapter 4.) However, the determination to feel and be united was not enough; the Nazis had to give public testimony to this "unity". The Nuremberg Rallies were carefully staged theatrical pieces devised to create such an effect. The mass political rally would continue to play a dominant role in the politics of the Third Reich where it was seen to be the physical manifestation of a nation's "triumph of the will". This also explains why the Nazis repeatedly staged "National Moments" ("*Stunden der Nation*") when Hitler's speeches would be broadcast simultaneously throughout the Reich. On such occasions life would come to a standstill, demonstrating the sense of national community where the individual participant in the ritual, moved by Hitler's rhetoric and swayed by the crowd, underwent a metamorphosis, in Goebbels' memorable phrase, "from a little worm into part of a large dragon".

CHAPTER THREE

The Führer state

Writing in his Memoirs, Hans Frank, the Nazi Governor-General of Poland, commented that Hitler had always been a Party man and he remained one as a statesman: "By the time of his investiture as Chancellor on 30 January 1933 he was the absolute autocrat of the NSDAP." According to Frank, the state apparatus with its formal lines of jurisdiction and hierarchies of authority was unfamiliar and strange to him. He felt inhibited and insecure towards it. Moreover the traditional form of legally ordered, formally independent, juridically controlled state executive represented constraints on his personal style of leadership. As the organizational form of the NSDAP had helped him secure victory and established his will as law within the Movement, he simply transferred the independent position he held within the Party and its inner structure to the state. The gradual erosion of collective government was to be replaced by the absolute power of the charismatic leader. The "Party of the Führer" would now be extended to become the "Führer state". This was to have profound implications for the government of the Third Reich.

The national community (*Volksgemeinschaft*)

From its very beginning, the Third Reich had set itself the ambitious task of "re-educating" the German people for a new society based upon what it saw as a "revolutionary" value system. Hitler had always rejected the liberal democracies that had evolved in most Western European countries by the beginning of the twentieth century. He fervently believed that the only salvation from the "degeneracy" of the Weimar Republic was the *Völkischer Staat* which would come about in Germany through a National Socialist type revolution. Coupled with this rejection of democracy was a belief that strong leadership (in the form of Hitler) was needed to transcend class and sectional interests and provide a new start. The Nazi slogan "Germany Awake" ("*Deutschland Erwache*") was intended to be a rallying call for a humiliated and weakened nation to rediscover its glorious past. Nazi propaganda made much of this. In a speech to a gathering of Nazi leaders in June 1933 Hitler claimed:

> The law of the National Socialist Revolution has yet to run its course. Its dynamic force still dominates development in Germany today, a development which presses forward irresistibly to a complete remodelling of German life ... Just as a magnet draws from a composite mass only the steel chips, so should a movement directed exclusively towards political struggle draw to itself only those natures which are called to a political leadership ... The German Revolution will not be complete until the whole German people has been fashioned anew, until it has been organised anew and has been reconstructed (Baynes 1942 vol. I: 481–3).

Having gained power, Hitler had no intention of allowing the traditional ruling elites to regain control. He was determined to consolidate and extend his powers. A central feature of the so-called "German Revolution" referred to above was Hitler's intention to radically restructure German society so that the prevailing class, religious and sectional loyalties would be replaced by a new heightened national awareness. In order to achieve this ambitious objective the Nazi regime would have to manipulate large masses of people and attempt to move them to uniformity of opinion and action. Hitler adopted a "carrot and stick" approach. Membership of an exclusive, racial-*völkisch* community was offered, while no opposition would be brooked from those unwilling to join, or deemed "undesirable". The pervasive fear of violence should not be underestimated, for it undoubtedly inhibited the forces of opposition. However, the menace of violence was, to some extent, counter-balanced by the positive image of new ethnic unity presented in the mass media on an unprecedented scale.

In order to manufacture a consensus where one did not previously exist, the Nazis urged the population to put "the community before the individual" (*Gemeinnutz vor Eigennutz*) and to place their faith in slogans like "One People! One Reich! One Führer!" The appeal to national ethnic unity based on a socially and racially homogeneous *Volksgemeinschaft* led by an all-knowing and benign Führer was intended to embrace most sections of society and set Germany apart from its European rivals (and also Marxist-Leninism). Hitler was presented in Nazi propaganda as a long-awaited messiah who would place the needs of his people before self-aggrandizement. The "charismatic" nature of his authority was dependent on his ability to convince a plebiscitory electorate of his "exemplary" character. For example, his celibacy, which was much debated, was explained in terms of his heroic "mission" for Germany and his determination to place the welfare of his subjects above personal happiness. To this end, the political function of propaganda was to co-ordinate the political will of the nation with the aims of the Leader and the State – or if this proved impossible with certain groups (for example, sections of the industrial working class and Bavarian Catholics), to establish at least passive acquiescence. Propaganda was intended to be the active force cementing the "national community" together, and the mass media – indeed art in general – would be used to *instruct* the people about the government's activities and why it required total support for the National Socialist State.

In the years leading up to the war – partly as an antidote to the increasing use of coercion and for the subsequent loss of liberty – propaganda eulogized the achievements of the regime. The press, radio, newsreels and film documentaries concentrated on the more prominent schemes: the impact of Nazi welfare services, Strength through Joy (the Labour Front's agency for programmed leisure), and Winter Aid. Posters proclaimed the benefits of "Socialism of the Deed", newsreels showed happy workers enjoying cruise holidays and visiting the "People's Theatre" for the first time, the radio bombarded the public's social conscience with charitable appeals, and the press stressed the value of belonging to a "national community" and the need for self-sacrifice in the interests of the state. The intention was to move away from social confrontation towards conciliation and integration. Cheap theatre and cinema tickets, along with cheap radio sets (*Volksempfänger*) and the cheap "People's Car" (*Volkswagen*), – even the "People's Court" (*Volksgerichtshof*) – were all intended to symbolize the achievements of the "people's community".

Closely linked to the idea of *Volksgemeinschaft* was the regime's desire to maintain social comformity. By creating a new series of public rituals to celebrate important days in the Nazi calendar, "national comrades" (*Volksgenossen*) were expected to attend parades and speeches and show their enthusiasm by hanging out flags. To integrate the people more fully into the community required positive and active devices that expressed publicly to Germans themselves and to the outside world, the national community in being. To this end the Nazis initiated the Winter Help (*Winterhilfe*) Programme for collecting money, food, and clothing for distressed families who had suffered as a result of mass unemployment. Secret Police reports suggest that during the first years of the regime *Winterhilfe* not only brought genuine relief to many but also functioned as a means of social integration by encouraging the more affluent members of society to aid the poor on the grounds of national and racial affinity. Similarly, the *Eintopf* ("one-pot") meal encouraged families once a month during the winter to have only one dish for their Sunday lunch and donate what they had saved to collectors who came to the door. Propaganda posters referred to the *Eintopf* as "the meal of sacrifice for the Reich" and urged all *Volksgenossen* to increase the size of their donations as a sign of their gratitude to the Führer. Rituals like Winter Help and the one-pot meal were intended to represent a vivid expression of the newly created "national community" and proof of loyalty to the regime. Increasingly, however, as unemployment ceased to be a problem and "voluntary" donations were diverted to pay for welfare measures and the rearmament programme, these compulsory gestures of conformity and "political reliability" met with widespread resentment to which the authorities responded with tough measures. Later, in the war, on the occasion of his anniversary address on 30 January 1942, Hitler referred to the collection campaigns as a "plebiscite", adding "While others talk about democracy, this *is* true democracy."

Propaganda presented an image of a society that had successfully manufactured a "national community" by transcending social and class divisiveness. But was there a gap between the Nazi propaganda image and social reality? Historians such as Tim Mason have suggested that there was, and indeed that the gap between social myth and social reality in the Third Reich grew ever wider. The argument suggests that propaganda of the "national community" failed to break down objective class and social divisions and more importantly failed to destroy an awareness of these divisions. The obvious danger of citing examples of social dissent (as opposed to resistance) is that this may be at the expense of stressing the significance of *Volksgemeinschaft* in terms of integration and stability (Welch 1995). That is not to say that "national community" propaganda sustained a heightened commitment to such a radical concept. The outbreak of war did eventually produce a decline in the standing of the Party (although Hitler's popularity only began to be affected from 1943 onwards), but German society did not fragment or disintegrate. Schemes like Strength through Joy, Winter Help, and the "One-Pot" meal could not be maintained indefinitely without resentment setting in. Equally, *Volksgemeinschaft* did not bring an end to people's grievances; they continued throughout the 12 years of the Third Reich. However, the implementation of a "people's community" was widely seen in positive terms that would continue to guarantee at least passive support for the regime. For the middle class it was perceived as an acceptable alternative to Marxist-Leninism and for workers it shifted the emphasis from a class-based appeal to one of nation. It may not have been recognized as a true "people's community" in the way in which it was eulogized in the mass media, but it was apparently tolerable to wide sections of the population (Welch 1995: 53).

Although, in my opinion, the *Volksgemeinschaft* represented more than merely a cosmetic exercise, it was never intended to embrace all Germans. The establishment of a socially and racially homogeneous "people's community" excluded many individuals and groups on grounds of race, political affiliation and health. Jews, Communists and Social Democrats, together with vagabonds, alcoholics and those with genetic diseases, were all deemed "outcasts" and excluded. Moreover, opposition was not simply discouraged, it was outlawed. As Martin Broszat has stated, "National Socialist justice" superseded the old *Rechtsstaat*. In 1928 Hitler had told an audience that "there is only one kind of law in this world and that lies in one's own strength". For Hitler, the law and the legal system was simply a means to an end. He spelt this out in unequivocal terms in his address to the Reichstag on the occasion of the Enabling Law of 23 March 1933:

Our legal system must, in the first place, serve to maintain this national community. The irremovability of the judges must, in the interests of society, be paralleled by an elasticity in sentencing. The nation rather than the individual must be regarded as the centre of the legal concern (Noakes & Pridham vol. 2 (1984): 475).

To this end, Hitler's power after 1933 was greatly enhanced by his control of the instruments of the coercive apparatus of the state. Alan Bullock has perceptively noted: "Hitler never abandoned the cloak of legality; he recognised the enormous psychological value of having the law on his side. Instead he turned the law inside out and made illegality legal" (Bullock 1952: 233). To oversimplify crudely, in modern capitalist democracies a "contract" exists whereby political and economic decisions are worked out through pluralist structures by elected governments and intermediary organizations by a process of dialogue, co-operation and consent. When this process breaks down, the pluralist structures collapse and decisions are imposed from above without consultation. The result is a form of state-imposed leadership that is invariably referred to as despotic or authoritarian. The Reichstag fire of 27 February 1933 had provided Hitler with the pretext to begin consolidating the foundations of an authoritarian one-party state, and the "enabling laws" forced through the Reichstag (referred to by the *Völkischer Beobachter* as the "capitulation of the parliamentary system to the new Germany") legalized intimidatory tactics and suspended civil rights in Germany.

The extraordinary achievement of the Nazis compared with other fascist and authoritarian regimes of the period was the speed with which they eliminated opposition. Within 18 months of coming to power they had erased all forms of political opposition by successfully preventing their opponents from organizing collectively. Within six months political opponents had been rounded up, incarcerated and outlawed. Within a year the quasi-autonomy of the regions had been crushed and in June 1934 the potential threat posed from within the Movement by the SA had been brutally eliminated in the "Night of the Long Knives". For individuals and groups that remained, a process of *Gleichschaltung* – by which all political, economic and cultural activities were assimilated within the state – ensured that a sufficient degree of conformity would sustain the regime in power until 1945.

Repression and fear generated during the first 18 months in office, together with the dissolution of independent organizations that had previously buffered the individuals and the state, partially explain the quiescence of the German population. The Nazi regime repressed its potential enemies with systematic thoroughness and brutality. Between 1933 and 1939 12,000 Germans were convicted of high treason. During the war a further 15,000 were condemned to death. It has been estimated, for example, that 30,000 members of the German Communist Party (KPD) were murdered by the Nazis and a further 300,000 sent to concentration camps (Gellately 1990). Of course there was dissent (mainly the result of cleavages that existed before 1933), but this occurs in one form or another in any political system during such a prolonged period in power. Such opposition as existed in Nazi Germany ("White Rose", the 1944 bomb plot on Hitler's life) remained isolated and was largely confined to grumblings about material conditions. While accepting that dictatorship gradually corrupts the moral fibre of its citizens and that resistance became increasingly difficult as the Nazi state consolidated its authority, one is nevertheless still left with the legitimate question: why was there so little resistance, particularly at the beginning? The reasons for the lack of co-ordinated protest are many and complex and outside the scope of this study. Suffice it to say that it is difficult to conceive, particularly after the death of President Hindenburg, of individuals or organizations able effectively to mount a challenge to Hitler or impose constraints on the increasing radicalization of Hitler's programmes. A small group of generals led by Ludwig Beck opposed Hitler's foreign policy in the late 1930s but were emasculated by France's and Britain's decision to appease Hitler over Czechoslovakia (see Chapter 4). The advent of the Second World War in 1939 made resistance even more difficult. In wartime any form of dissident behaviour can be construed as violating the patriotic duty of allegiance owed to one's country. Not surprisingly the number of treasonable offences increased from three to 46 and over 15,000 such sentences were handed out during the war.

The image of an ordered and disciplined society strongly led and united behind its leader is the image that Nazi propaganda wished to convey. In fact the reality was very different. According to Otto Dietrich, Hitler's Press Chief, Hitler produced "the biggest confusion in government that has ever existed in a civilised state". It would be no exaggeration to use the metaphor of feudal anarchy to describe the system of government during the Third Reich. Jeremy Noakes has referred to it as a "labyrinthine structure of overlapping competencies, institutional confusion and a chaos of personal rivalries" (Noakes & Pridham vol. 2 (1984): 204). The traditional view, then, of the Nazi regime being a monolithic power structure has been largely rejected and replaced by a more critical, polycratic model, based on the shapelessness, lack of clear direction, and improvization of Nazi rule. The chief explanation for this state of affairs is the attitude and personality of Hitler himself and the style of leadership developed within the Nazi Party before 1933. Most historians today would agree on the centrality of Hitler to the phenomenon of Nazism – indeed, it is almost impossible to conceive of the Third Reich without him. It is equally difficult to imagine that the regime would have been able to reproduce itself after the death of Hitler (unlike, for example, the Soviet Union, after the death of Stalin). Crucial, therefore, to an understanding of the nature of the Third Reich is the impact on government of Hitler's ideological "visions" and his equally personal style of charismatic leadership. Historians continue to disagree, however, over whether or not Hitler was a "programmatist" consistently pursuing defined ideological objectives. What is agreed is that within the Nazi Movement, Hitler's status was based on the *Führerprinzip* and that this mythical notion of leadership formed one of the unwavering planks of the Nazi *Weltanschauung*.

Hitler and charismatic leadership (*Führerprinzip*)

For their concept of the heroic leader the nazis turned once again to *völkisch* thought and the notion of *Führerprinzip*, of a mystical figure embodying and guiding the nation's destiny. In practical terms this meant that decisions came down from above instead of being worked out by discussion and choice from below. The roots and antecedents of such a concept are more complex and derive from many sources: the messianic principle of Christianity, the thaumaturgic kings of the Middle Ages, the Nietzschean "superman" of *völkisch* mythology, and rightist circles in Germany before the First World War. However, the Nazi belief in the *Führerprinzip*, as it found expression in Germany after 1933, stemmed partly from the distaste which Germans felt towards the nineteenth century for the determining of policy by the counting of votes, and partly from the way in which Nazi philosophers such as Alfred Bäumler had reinterpreted Nietzsche's concept of the "triumph of the will" by individual genius. The *Führerprinzip* was to be based on a very special personality which had the will and power to actualize the *Volksstaat*. This would be achieved by the man of destiny – resolute, uncompromising, dynamic and radical – who would destroy the old privileged and class-ridden society and replace it by the ethnically pure and socially harmonious "national community". By implication it would be the antithesis of democracy. The extreme fragmentation of Weimar politics, which were increasingly seen in terms of a failure to govern, served only to make such leadership qualities appear all the more attractive.

The cult of the leader, which surpassed any normal level of trust in political leadership, is central to an understanding of the appeal of National Socialism, and undoubtedly the most important theme cementing Nazi propaganda together. In his study *Behemoth*, which was published in 1942, Franz Neumann pointed out that the Third Reich was no totalitarian dictatorship in the sense of a "monolithic, authoritarian system inspired by a unified policy". Neumann argued that despite all the revolutionary slogans, the old social order and traditional ruling class remained. Neumann attempted to show that the Nazi regime had created a form of direct rule over the suppressed masses, which was without any rational legality and which was dependent upon four largely autonomous groups, each pressing its own administrative and legal powers. These were the Party, the army, the bureaucracy, and industry. (Had he written the book when more information was available he would surely have included the SS.) But towering above all the rival groups was the symbolic figure of the Führer, the head of state who was not subject to any constitutional checks and balances.

Following the "seizure of power", the authority associated with charismatic leadership was transferred from the National Socialist Party to the German state and nation. On 19 August 1934, following a plebiscite supported by 89.9 per cent (95.7 per cent of the 45 million eligible voters went to the polls), the law concerning the head of state of the German Reich merged the offices of Reich President and Reich Chancellor into the new office of "Führer and Reich Chancellor" which became very quickly abbreviated to "Führer". Although

Hitler's position was now defined in constitutional terms, the nature of charismatic leadership led to what has been called a polycratic system of government where the traditional spheres of authority, like the state and the legal system, operated side-by-side with the more abstract notion of "Führer-power" (*Führergewalt*), which was exclusive and unlimited. Ernst Huber, the Nazi political theorist, defined such power as follows:

> The position of Führer combines in itself all sovereign power of the Reich; all public power in the State as in the movement is derived from the Führer power. If we wish to define political power in the *völkisch* Reich correctly, we must not speak of "State power" but of "Führer power". For it is not the State as an impersonal entity which is the source of political power but rather political power is given to the Führer as the executor of the nation's common will. Führer power is comprehensive and total; it unites within itself all means of creative political activity; it embraces all spheres of national life; it includes all national comrades who are bound to the Führer in loyalty and obedience. Führer power is not restricted by safeguards and controls, by autonomous protected spheres, and by vested individual rights, but rather it is free and independent, exclusive and unlimited (Noakes & Pridham vol. 2 (1984): 199).

"Führer-power" operated at a number of different levels. For disparate activists within the NSDAP, Hitler, as undisputed Führer, represented the unifying force of the Movement. Embodied in the notion of the *Führerprinzip* was a recognition on the part of all the different interests within the Party of where power resided. As such the *Führerprinzip* governed the organizational structure of Nazism and provided it with its unique source of legitimacy. For the mass population who were not Party members, on the other hand, Hitler filled a vacuum caused by the sudden loss of the monarchy in 1918. Nazi propaganda presented him as a contemporary *Volkskaiser* who transcended party politics, but a leader who demanded unconditional loyalty and obedience in order to bring about the *Volksgemeinschaft*. This mass recognition proved particularly important in persuading non-Nazi elites to accept Hitler's authority in the crucial transitory period immediately after the "seizure of power".

While in theory the Weimar Constitution was never abrogated, Hitler's position as Führer and exclusive representative of the nation's will was quickly consolidated. In order to achieve this position of unrestricted power, the Nazi state intimidated a judiciary which sanctioned what was happening and by its total subservience to the "will of the Führer" removed its traditional function as an independent third force of the state. Although few changes were made to civil law, the Nazis proved ruthlessly opportunistic in utilizing the criminal law for their own ends. By gradually subverting legal norms to executive SS-police action acting under the guise of Führer-power, the Nazis could rely on the compliance of a national-conservative judiciary who had remained hostile to the liberal principles of the Weimar Republic which had protected individual rights against excesses of the state. Therefore, without necessarily being staunch Nazis, many judges and lawyers welcomed the Nazi regime in 1933 for its promise to restore a more authoritarian notion of "law and order" and, by implication, the status of the judiciary.

Led by Reich Minister of Justice, Franz Gürtner (who was not a Nazi), the erosion of legality began shortly after the Reichstag fire, when the Decree for the Protection of the People and the State (passed on 29 March 1933) retrospectively imposed the death penalty on van der Lubbe for allegedly setting fire to the Reichstag, even though the death penalty for arson had not existed at the time of the offence. In fact the "Reichstag Fire Decree" (as it was popularly known) was used indiscriminately to arrest any political opponent of Nazism who could now be interned without trial. Whereas 268 cases were tried for high treason in 1932, in 1933 the figure had risen to over 11,000. In March 1933, in order to deal with treason trials resulting from the "Lex van der Lubbe", a new system of Special Courts, operating without juries, was introduced. It was Gürtner who also gave legal sanction to the massacre of the SA leadership in June 1934 ("Night of the Long Knives") by claiming that the state had "anticipated" treasonable action and that the measures were justified on the grounds of self-defence. The progressive erosion of the rule of law and the old *Rechtstaat* was further undermined by the setting up in April 1934 of the so-called People's Court (*Volksgerichtshof*) to deal with cases of treason. Many Party purists hoped that the People's Court would become the direct expression of a *völkisch* concept of the law. Staffed by five judges, only two of whom needed to be lawyers, and using juries made up only of Party officials, the People's Court denied defendants most of their rights, including that of appeal against a verdict. By 1937, however, the People's Court found itself increasingly supplanted by the massive expansion in the power of the merged police and SS who were operating outside the conventional framework of the law as a direct executive organ of the "Führer's will".

The basis for the interpretation of all laws was now the National Socialist philosophy, as expressed in the Party programme, the speeches of the Führer and "healthy popular feelings". Carl Schmidt, a constitutional lawyer, defined the principles of Nazi law as simply "a spontaneous emanation of the Führer's will". This view was made quite explicit in a speech made by Hans Frank, the head of the Nazi Association of Lawyers and of the Academy of German Law, in 1938:

1. At the head of the Reich stands the leader of the NSDAP as leader of the German Reich for life.
2. He is, on the strength of his being leader of the NSDAP, leader and Chancellor of the Reich. As such he embodies simultaneously, as Head of State, supreme State power and, as chief of the Government, the central functions of the whole Reich administration. He is Head of State and chief of the Government in one person. He is Commander-in-Chief of all the armed forces of the Reich.
3. The Führer and Reich Chancellor is the constituent delegate of the German people, who without regard for formal preconditions decides the outward form of the Reich, its structure and general policy.
4. The Führer is supreme judge of the nation ... There is no position in the area of constitutional law in the Third Reich independent of this elemental will of the Führer ...

The Führer is not backed by constitutional clauses, but by outstanding achievements which are based on the combination of a calling and of his devotion to the people ... Whether the Führer governs according to a formal written Constitution is not a legal question ... The legal question is only whether through his activity the Führer guarantees the existence of his people (Noakes & Pridham vol. 2 (1984): 199–200).

Thus Hitler's position of absolute power was justified not in legal-rational terms as Chancellor and Head of State but in charismatic terms as Führer of the German *Volk* – not a state, but a German nation as a racially-determined entity. As the custodian of the nation's will, constitutional limitations could not be imposed on his authority. The legal system and individual judges had no right to question the decisions of the Führer, which were increasingly disguised as laws or decrees, and thus given the facade of normality. Such "normality" could, however, be violated at any time by individuals or organizations, for example the Gestapo, who could claim to be operating within the sphere of Führer-power. In this way the constitutional state was delivered into the hands of the "healthy feelings of the nation" which, it was claimed, would generate the strength and energy necessary for national revival and Germany's quest to become a dominant world power.

Implicit in this transfer of power was a recognition that traditional individual rights and civil liberties would be suspended. An example of how this insidiously manifested itself is the following report by the *Guardian* newspaper in December 1934. Nazi officials were apparently incensed at the widespread refusal to reciprocate the "Hitler Salute" (when a salute is given, the words "Heil Hitler'" are spoken and the right hand is raised – the salute is then returned in the same manner). Officials in Berlin complained that workers were "scandalously" failing to return the appropriate salute and in future would be reported. A warning was issued in terms that encapsulate what it must have been like for ordinary citizens confronted with the inquisitorial mentality of petty Party officials in the Führer state:

> Fellow-countryman! Do not obstruct! It is necessary to show our Führer Adolf Hitler, who has suffered so infinitely for the German people and has done so much for them, the respect which is due because of his deeds for the whole of the German people. Whoever obstructs thereby places himself outside the German community and will be valued and treated accordingly. Heil Hitler! (*Guardian*, 5 December 1934).

In attempting to assess the relationship between the people and the Nazi regime, I have argued elsewhere (Welch, 1995) that Hitler achieved a remarkable degree of consensus over a 12-year period and

enjoyed genuine popular support for many of his policies. Membership of his Party increased by 200 per cent in his first year of office and
by 1939 the NSDAP boasted a membership of five million. Although
elections and plebiscites tended to be rigged and the media tightly
controlled, it would not be strictly true to say that public opinion
ceased to exist. Hitler was acutely aware of the constant need to
gauge public moods and regularly received detailed feedback reports
from the public opinion and morale gathering agencies. His recorded
determination in 1935–6, for example, to avoid increasing food prices
at all costs for fear that this would undermine his popularity suggests
a political sensitivity to public opinion. To assure himself of continued popular support was an unwavering concern of Hitler's.

To this end a number of different agencies were engaged in assessing the state of public opinion and the factors affecting public morale.
The Security Service (SD), the Gestapo, the Party, local government
authorities and the judiciary all made it their business to gauge the
mood and morale of the people. Their reports were based on information received from agents throughout the Reich, who reported
on their conversations with Party members or on conversations they
had overheard. It has been estimated that by 1939 the SD alone had
some 3,000 full-time officials and some 50,000 part-time agents. This
desire to know what people were thinking and how they were acting
had, of course, profound implications. The knowledge that spying of
this magnitude existed would certainly have shaped attitudes towards
the regime. The extent to which Nazi authorities intruded into every
aspect of life in the Third Reich is well documented and went far
beyond punishment for failing to provide the appropriate Hitler
salute. Children and students were encouraged to denounce parents
or teachers with dissident opinions, neighbours were to inform the
Gestapo of suspicious behaviour, parishioners to expose the clergy.
Spying was endemic and for many "ordinary" citizens it became a
way of demonstrating loyalty to the Führer, obtaining personal
advancement, and settling old scores. It should never be forgotten
that fear and terror were always at the back of such a "consensus".
To dissent (or "resist") in private risked fear of denunciation, to
demonstrate in public warranted incarceration in concentration
camps.

Nevertheless, in spite of the terror and the disregard for civil
liberties, it would still be an oversimplification to think of the

German public as a *tabula rasa* upon which Hitler drew whatever picture he wished. In any political system policy must be explained, and the public must either be convinced of the efficacy of government decisions or at least remain indifferent to them. Nazi Germany was no exception, and as with any other political system, public opinion and propaganda remained inexorably linked. That is not to say that all major decisions taken by Hitler were influenced by public opinion. Such a statement is clearly absurd; rather, decision-making and the propaganda justifying policy were conditioned by an awareness of how the public felt about certain issues.

Hitler's style of leadership

The *Führerprinzip* laid down that at all levels of organization, ultimate authority was concentrated in a single leader imbued with special gifts. This authority remained absolute. In theory this designated simple official hierarchies of authority like a chain of command in a military structure. Hitler gave orders and these were transmitted down and carried out by the relevant authorities. In practice it was far more complex and confusing ("untidy" would be a better description). Students of political history comparing different forms of totalitarian government invariably refer to "systems". This is not entirely appropriate when thinking about Nazi rule – although it is understandable. Ian Kershaw has reminded us that, in the case of the Third Reich, it is more accurate to think of it in terms of "systemlessness" chaos in which anything resembling a state *system* based on rational order of government rapidly disintegrated (Kershaw 1993: 107). Jeremy Noakes (using Max Weber's terminology) has referred to the nature of Nazi rule as a peculiar combination of charisma and bureaucracy (Noakes & Pridham vol. 2 (1984): 198). One explanation for this state of affairs is that Hitler consciously established independent hierarchies of authority at both Party and state level that depended on the Führer to confirm their authority. He was able, therefore, to deploy a policy of "divide and rule" in order that no single organization threatened his position. Hitler on the other hand was not bound by such constraints and would invariably operate outside the official hierarchical structures whenever he chose. Thus obscure and confusing channels of communications evolved through which information and power flowed to and from Hitler from a plethora of competing channels that did not stand in any hierarchical relationship to one another. This labyrinthine chaos is partially explained by the manner in which leadership developed within the NSDAP before 1933 and also by the unwillingness on the part of Hitler to resolve the Party/state dualism.

As we have seen in Chapter 1, by 1932 the NSDAP had been restructured by Hitler for the purpose of propaganda and winning elections (one could argue that Hitler was also essentially a propagandist). The Party did not possess the organizational structures to administer a modern state and Hitler lacked the awareness of the problems involved in converting propaganda slogans into policy and action. Moreover the *Führerprinzip* prevented the development of bureaucratic-rational delineations of authority below the position of the leader (Geary 1993: 45). Hitler's unchallenged position as dictator within the Party had been cultivated on the principles of personal loyalty and devoted commitment to the Führer. Once in power, the Party's *ad hoc* organizational structure, based on a combination of bureaucracy and charisma, was "bolted on" to the existing hierarchical structures of the state. Thus the potential for rivalry below the level of Hitler, which was implicit in the "systemless" organizational structure of the NSDAP, was to become even more acute in the Third Reich as subordinates in both Party and state organizations clamoured for Hitler's favours. A *Gau* (district) leader, for example, who had access to Hitler, was more important than a Reich Minister who may rarely have had contact with his head of state. (The unconventional nature of status in the Third Reich is illustrated by the fact that Hitler's chauffeurs became high dignitaries of the regime and were given a general's rank!) As cabinet meetings virtually ceased after 1937, certain ministers in charge of departments might for months on end, and even for years, have no opportunity of speaking to Hitler. Thus Hitler's personal position involved an extraordinary claim to omnipotence and also omniscience. So as to strengthen his own unique position Hitler would play Party against state in order to "divide and rule" and the gradual erosion of constitutional checks and balances served to faciliate this process and increase his power and authority.

In a pluralist society, state officials working, for example, in a government department would be answerable to a minister. Under the *Führerprinzip*, however, they were encouraged to view themselves as Hitler's direct representatives and thus their first responsibility was to the Führer. Such a system undermined Ministerial authority. By playing individuals and organizations against one another, Hitler progressively corroded the historical basis of the German state which, in turn, led to the proliferation of polycratic agencies subject only to Führer-power. Hitler is therefore largely responsible for sustaining the irreconcilable dualism of Party and state that existed at every level and undermined effective government and corrupted public life.

The official hierarchies of authority were further complicated by the numerous bodies set up by Hitler and responsible directly to him. To deal with special problems, Hitler established *ad hoc* institutions independent of Party and state bureaucracy, which invariably became permanent. A typical example of this is Göring's Office of the Four-Year Plan. By 1936 Hitler had become incensed with the economic crisis and the stance adopted by his Economics Minister, Hjalmar Schacht, and sections of big business. Although he rarely put pen to paper himself (other than to sign decrees) he felt compelled on this occasion to draft a secret Four-Year Plan Memorandum intended to prepare the German economy for war and effectively handed over control of the economy to Göring and the new Office which rapidly built up a massive organizational empire employing over a thousand officials. At the time only two copies of this major policy document were distributed (to Göring and to Minister for War, Field Marshal Werner von Blomberg). Revealingly, Schacht, the Minister for Economics, was not included on the distribution list.

Thus a tripartite structure emerged whereby government departments would exist side-by-side with Party-controlled institutions and *ad hoc* bodies set up to deal with issues that had a specific resonance for Hitler. For example, the Todt Organization (later taken over by Albert Speer) was responsible for public works, Baldur von Schirach was given responsibiity for mobilizing German youth under the banner of the Hitler Youth, and infamously the huge empire of the SS headed by Heinrich Himmler and Reinhard Heydrich was charged with "safeguarding the ... embodiment of the National Socialist idea" including responsibility for the concentration camps. During the war these special agencies increased their power enormously, constrained by very few rules and answerable only to Hitler who remained indifferent to the methods they employed so long as the broad objectives which he had set out were achieved.

This extraordinary state of affairs, whereby the more powerful Nazi "warlords" were left free to build up their rival empires and even to feud with each other, reflected Hitler's racial belief in the survival of the fittest. In *Mein Kampf* Hitler had written: "Men dispossess one another and one perceives at the end of it all it is always the stronger who triumphs. The stronger asserts his will. It is the law of nature." Hitler's social Darwinism led him to conclude that if he allowed the law of the jungle to prevail in his own government, the strongest would emerge and he could then support the victor. Hitler was therefore encouraging conflict by creating new institutions in a struggle for the survival of the fittest. The result has been variously described as "authoritarian anarchy", "administrative chaos", and "permanent improvisation" – certainly a far cry from the picture-book monolithic, totalitarian state that the Nazis projected in their propaganda (Bullock 1995: 11).

It is difficult to conceive of a style of leadership that was more incompatible with modern rational decision-making. Hitler systematically disorganized the machinery of government. He certainly destroyed collective, centralized government. Until the death of Hindenburg in August 1934, Hitler appears to have been a punctilious Chancellor discharging his duties in the manner expected of him by the ailing Hindenburg. According to one of his adjutants, Fritz Wiedemann, this fairly orderly regime broke down after the General's death when Hitler reverted to a lifestyle not dissimilar to that of the party leader of the 1920s:

> Later Hitler normally appeared shortly before lunch, read quickly through Reich Press Chief Dietrich's press cuttings, and then went to lunch. So it became more and more difficult for Lammers [head of the Reich Chancellery] and Meissner [State Secretary] to get him to make decisions which he alone could make as Head of State.... When Hitler stayed at Obersalzberg it was even worse. There, he never left his room before 2.00 p.m. Then, he went to lunch. He spent most afternoons taking a walk, in the evening straight after dinner, there were films. There can be no question of Hitler's work habits being similar to those attributed to Frederick the Great or Napoleon. He disliked the study of documents. I have sometimes secured decisions from him, even ones about important matters, without his ever asking

to see the relevant files. He took the view that many things sorted themselves out on their own if one did not interfere (Noakes and Pridham vol. 2 (1984): 207–8).

Compared with an interventionist dictator like Stalin who would constantly interfere with policy with a stream of directives, Hitler detested administration to do with domestic policy, preferring to galvanize subordinates with a combination of inspiration and intimidation. Increasingly he began to absent himself from his Chancellery, spending long weekends in his Berchtesgaden retreat away from the German capital, Berlin. Until 1935, Heinrich Lammers, head of the Reich Chancellery, and therefore the only formal link between Hitler and his ministers, managed to see Hitler regularly. However, despite an office of the Reich Chancellery having been opened in Berchtesgaden so that Lammers could be near Hitler, he still had no right of access to the Führer, who would often ignore his requests for regular meetings. As Hitler was averse to paperwork, attending committees or chairing cabinet meetings, the most usual form of contact was through face-to-face contact with ministers and subordinates, of which few records were kept. In the absence of agendas and minutes of meetings, Hitler's "directives" (which were often short and abrupt) assumed delphic proportions. Therefore the key to gaining and maintaining power within one's sphere of influences was the ability to convince people that one was operating with the blessing of the Führer. To do this one had to gain access to Hitler. Not surprisingly a vacuum emerged between the top level of political power, the "superministerial" structures corresponding to the extremely personal character of this kind of contact with Hitler, and lower Reich ministers who did not belong to this privileged group and who were sinking to the level of mere civil servants. Hugh Trevor-Roper pointed out some years ago that Hitler's government had more in common with a medieval court than a twentieth-century cabinet or presidential government.

The fragmentary and complex nature of the administrative structure is further illustrated by the role (or lack of it) of the Reich Chancellery. The *Führerprinzip* meant that the cabinet was never the final source of authority. As supreme authority and sole arbiter of state and Party, Hitler did not exactly encourage open debate on policy matters. Even as Party leader Hitler had never been interested in debate, taking criticism on a very personal level. Ernst Nolte has referred to this as the trait of infantilism in Hitler's nature. The whole point of the *Führerprinzip* and "charismatic authority" was to dissolve opposition and structures that might have imposed rational constraints on Hitler's "heroic mission". There were 12 cabinet meetings in 1935, four in 1936 and six in 1937. The last cabinet meeting was held in February 1938. Although the influence of the Reich Chancellery briefly increased as it replaced the cabinet, it had no formal role in the policy-making process and Lammers' power, as we have seen, was strictly limited. Thus the decision-making process was rarely co-ordinated and as there were no clear-cut channels of command, Hitler remained unchallenged. He preferred, instead, to allow his trusty henchmen (Göring, Goebbels, Himmler, Bormann) to compete against each other for power and influence, since para-doxically this could strengthen his own position as Führer. In so doing they were also undermining the basis on which the state and legal order in Germany had existed for over one hundred years. When Reich Interior Minister Frick attempted to rationalize the haphazard nature of the administration his efforts were constantly thwarted by Hitler who invariably sided with the objections raised by his Gauleiters. Ernst von Weizsäcker, State Secretary in the Foreign Office, provided a revealing anecdote on Hitler's style of leadership:

> Ministerial skill in the Third Reich consisted in making the most of a favourable hour or minute when Hitler made a decision, this often taking the form of a remark thrown out casually, which then went its way as an "Order of the Führer" (Weizsäcker 1951: 164).

Having dispensed with the cabinet and undermined the Reich Chancellery, Hitler chose the company of an inner circle of confi-dantes within which criticism was unknown and intellectual exchange impossible as visitors were expected to listen to Hitler's rambling monologues. Writing in his memoirs after the war, Baldur von Schirach suggested that this sycophancy bolstered Hitler's increasing detachment from reality: "this unlimited, almost religious veneration, to which I contributed as did Goebbels, Göring, Hess, Ley, and countless others, strengthened in Hitler himself the belief that he was in league with Providence" (quoted Kershaw 1987: 263). In this context, the Office of the Staff of the Führer's Deputy, created in 1933 and renamed the Party Chancellery in 1941 following Rudolf Hess's flight to Scotland, provides an important insight into the nature of the regime and Hitler's style of leadership. Martin Bormann, who replaced Hess, has remained a shadowy figure. By 1935 Bormann had made himself almost indispensable; he had taken over from Hess the role of Hitler's unofficial secretary, he had acquired control of the Obersalzberg estate and had, unlike Lammers, gained regular access to Hitler. Bormann seized these opportunities and exploited them to the full, increasing his own power in the process. Bormann, who was a fierce guardian of Nazi orthodoxy, proved also to be a tireless and skilful political manipulator. Lacking the intellectual substance to develop a distinctive political vision of his own, Bormann exploited his position of trust to defend the Party's interest and to shield Hitler from the burdens of war by cocooning him in an artificial world populated by "yes-men" guaranteed to massage Hitler's increasingly megalomanic fantasies. In turn, Hitler regarded him as an indispensable aid – so much so that in his last will and testament Hitler named Bormann ("my loyal Party Comrade") as his executor.

Goebbels, on the other hand, was not so impressed and attempted to undermine Bormann's apparent hold over Hitler. After the first serious military setback at Stalingrad in the winter of 1942–3 an exhausted Hitler had been repeatedly shielded by Bormann from facing fundamentally difficult decisions. Between January and August 1943 Hitler met on 11 occasions with the so-called "Committee of Three" comprising Bormann, Lammers and Field Marshal Keitel. Goebbels, Speer, Göring and others who had been excluded from this inner circle attempted to undermine the committee (referred to by Goebbels as "this evil trio"). They proposed setting up a Defence Council of Ministers that would advise Hitler, administer the nation's domestic affairs, restructure defence policy and generally place the country on a total-war footing. The arbitrary nature of Hitler's government and the intense personal rivalries that developed out of it ensured that the "Committee of Three" faded as a form of collective government and the demands of the "conspirators" to unify and co-ordinate the country's administration were blocked by a prevaricating Hitler who continued to view the complete mobilization of the home front as an admission of defeat.

Bormann's Party Chancellery derived its authority from its claim to be the conduit of the Führer's will in both Party matters and the affairs of state. It concentrated above all on issues central to Nazi ideology: the Jews, population policy and the churches (a particular crusade for Bormann who regarded Christianity as a major obstacle to the one-party dictatorship). The role of the Party Chancellery appears to have been one of transforming already existing ideas into action rather than taking independent initiatives. That is not to suggest that the Party Chancellery did not attempt to break loose from these limits. Bormann's office often pressed for a radicalizaton of policy in ideologically important areas. Although it is claimed that by the end of the war Bormann had become second only to Hitler in terms of real political power, recent research by Peter Longerich has suggested that Bormann's power has been overestimated and that he was never able to achieve dominance over the competing claims of rivals such as Göring, Himmler, Goebbels and Speer. Nevertheless, Bormann continued to assert the authority of the Party Chancellery over rival fiefdoms. The in-built contradictions that existed between the charismatic and bureaucratic dynamics of the regime ultimately circumscribed the Party Chancellery as it did any other ministry or agency. Referred to misleadingly by some historians as "Hitler's Mephistopheles", Bormann undoubtedly reinforced orthodox Nazi ideological tendencies in the direction of greater radicalization but in *realpolitik* terms his authority ultimately rested on the basis of representing the Führer's will.

The *Führerprinzip* and the manner in which Hitler's style of leadership developed were incompatible with a modern rational decision-making government. During the war the strains imposed by such *ad hoc* "structures" resulted in increasing chaos. The proliferation of competing "polycratic" authorities is one thing within a political party established for propaganda purposes; it is very different when such a "systemless" structure is imposed on a modern state. The result was a "Führer-state". It was not the efficient well-managed and structured government of Nazi propaganda. The reality behind the propaganda was a ramshackle collection of competing fiefdoms with Hitler as the final, and sometimes hesitant, arbiter.

The behaviour and personality of Hitler together with the form of leadership developed within the Party prior to 1933 became major factors in the style and content of government after 1933. Hitler certainly applied a radically different conception of government to anything seen in Germany before. A paradox lies at the heart of Hitler's rule. On the one hand the Führer was all powerful, supported by huge plebiscites and unconstrained by parliamentary checks and balances, yet on the other hand he was rarely involved in the day-to-day affairs of state. Interventions, when they did occur, were usually at the behest of privileged officials who had gained access to the Führer. Hitler was simply bored with the day-to-day minutiae of domestic affairs and government paperwork. This was not a conscious policy of leadership whereby he was loath to intervene – he simply could not be bothered. According to his adjutant, Fritz Wiedemann, Hitler "took the view that many things sorted themselves out on their own if one did not interfere". The exception to this rule, when he was never slow to intervene, was if he thought his own position was being threatened. But generally at the heart of Hitler's personality was a vast vacuum of disinterest in day-to-day affairs. This combination of ambition, energy and indolence has been referred to already. The two notable exceptions where Hitler continued to take a leading interest in order to secure the implementation of his ideological fixations were the acquisition of *Lebensraum* ("living space") in the east and the "solution" to the "Jewish Question". My intention is to analyze these two central planks of Hitler's *Weltanschauung* in some detail and ask how these "fixations" were translated into policy.

CHAPTER FOUR

Hitler's road to war

When Britain and France declared war on Germany on 3 September 1939, Hitler's foreign policy vision, which had remained constant since the mid 1920s, appeared to be in tatters. In *Mein Kampf* and the *Second book*, Hitler had argued that Germany should develop an entente with Britain, the nation he most admired. Instead, he was now at war with Britain (France was an implacable foe) and allied to his ideological enemy, the Soviet Union, the country he had always despised. How can this apparent volte-face be explained? The first point to note is that despite the image of a strong leader, Hitler had always found it difficult to make up his mind in times of crisis. In 1932 he almost lost the Chancellorship; in June 1934 Hitler agreed to the purge of the SA ("Night of the Long Knives") only belatedly and reluctantly; he shelved dealing with the economic crisis of 1935–6, when a serious shortage of raw materials and foodstuffs arose; and in September 1938 Hitler almost lost his nerve in the Sudetenland crisis. As has already been mentioned, Hitler's style of leadership had led to a chaotic form of administrative anarchy. It is not surprising to discover, therefore, that his foreign policy, governed as it was by a combination of ideology, opportunism and instinct, should be equally inconsistent and contradictory. In fact Hitler never lost sight of his utopian vision of a Greater Germanic Reich, and even on the eve of the outbreak of the Second World War he still hoped that an agreement could be reached with Britain allowing Germany a free hand to expand eastwards. It was the effete democracies who were opposing his territorial ambitions and thus refusing to play the game according to his blueprint. The gamble that Hitler undertook in 1939 inevitably led to a collision course with the Western powers and the dynamics implicit in his utopian vision drove him relentlessly from one conquest to the next in pursuit of world power status.

In one of Hitler's first speeches on foreign policy in May 1933 he talked about about righting the wrongs of Versailles. In October he took a significant decision which represented a break with past policy and withdrew Germany from the Geneva Disarmament Conference and the League of Nations. Overturning the Versailles Treaty attracted widespread support within Germany and considerable tacit support outside. Indeed, by 1933, Germany had stopped paying reparations and a number of the Treaty's punitive articles had either been ignored or dismantled. In 1934 he steered a new course of *rapprochement* with Poland that resulted in a non-aggression treaty. This represented a surprising piece of diplomacy on Hitler's part and was undertaken against the advice of a number of his leading politicians and diplomats. In 1936 when Hitler ordered German troops into the demilitarized Rhineland there was little international protest, while Germans saw it as a sign that the nation was regaining self-respect. Few in Germany bothered to read *Mein Kampf* to discover Hitler's real motives and his obsession with territorial expansion. Nazi propaganda portrayed Hitler as a man of peace pursuing justifiable revisions of the humiliating Versailles Treaty.

The treaty that led to the Rome–Berlin Axis in November 1936 had changed the balance of power in Europe, and Austria, in particular, was left isolated as a result. Previously, Austria had depended on an alliance between Britain, France and Italy to secure her independence in the face of German demands. With Italy now on Germany's side, the balance of power in central Europe had shifted dramatically. In February 1938, Hitler summoned the Austrian Chancellor Kurt von Schuschnigg and increased the pressure on the Austrian government to include a Nazi nominee in the cabinet. Schuschnigg had been worried by increased Nazi activity in Austria and had come to Germany hoping to secure assistance from Hitler. Austrian Nazis had, in fact, attempted an earlier coup in 1934 with the assassination of Chancellor Dollfuss. On that occasion they were thwarted by Mussolini who opposed German intervention in Austria. As a result of the Rome–Berlin Axis, Hitler was now in a stronger position, and in the meeting with Schuschnigg insisted on far-reaching demands, which the Austrian Chancellor at first accepted. On 9 March, how-ever, Schuschnigg announced a plebiscite to decide on Austria's fate, confident that the people would vote to remain independent. Schuschnigg's initiative forced Hitler to act and on 12 March 1938, German troops crossed the border and Austria was declared part of the German Reich. The German invasion of Austria was Hitler's first move outside German territory in defiance of the Treaty of Versailles. Shortly afterwards a plebiscite was arranged so effectively in both Germany and Austria that 99 per cent of those voting supported Hitler's actions. Austria was relegated to a mere province of the Reich. "For me", Hitler informed the press, "this is the proudest hour of my life."

The *Anschluss* of Austria not only revealed the extent of Hitler's imperial ambitions, it also dealt a strategic blow at Czechoslovakia which could now be attacked from the south as well as from the west and north. The Republic of Czechoslovakia had been created in 1918 and contained a volatile racial mix of Czechs, Slovaks, Hungarians, Ruthenes, and some three million Germans mostly living in the Sudetenland. Nevertheless, it had shown itself to be more genuinely democratic than many of its neighbours. Hitler, however, decided to use the grievances of the German minority led by Konrad Henlein as a pretext for his expansionist ambitions.

When Neville Chamberlain became British Prime Minister in May 1937 he gave a new impetus to appeasement. For Chamberlain, appeasement meant taking the initiative and showing Hitler that "reasonable" claims could be achieved by negotiation and not force. Chamberlain and Daladier, the new French Prime Minister, feared that the Czech crisis could precipitate a wider conflict and decided that Czechoslovakia was simply not worth a European war. The Czechoslovak President, Beneš, was urged therefore to make concessions to the Sudeten Germans. Chamberlain had three meetings with Hitler: at Berchtesgaden on 15 September, at Bad Godesberg on 22–23 September, and at Munich on 29–30 September. At the first meeting, Hitler stated his intention to annex the Sudetenland on the principle of self-determination. At Bad Godesberg he insisted on immediate German occupation, and finally at Munich he was persuaded to accept a phased occupation with an international commission to arbitrate over disputed boundaries.

As President Beneš, urged on by Britain and France, offered the Sudeten Germans wider measures of autonomy, Henlein was instructed to "demand so much that we can never be satisfied". On 29

September 1938, an international conference was held at Munich. The participants were Germany, Italy, Britain and France. Conspicuous by their absence were Czechoslovakia, whose fate was to be decided, and the Soviet Union, which was not invited. At Munich a number of deals were struck at the expense of Czechoslovak sovereignty. The agreement, signed on 30 September, stipulated that the Germans were to occupy the Sudetenland between 1 and 10 October and the four powers together with Czechoslovakia were to form a commission which was to supervise the takeover and deal with any disputes arising from the agreement. An annexe to the agreement stated that once the Polish and Hungarian claims had been settled the rump state of Czechoslovakia was to be guaranteed by the four powers. Later that day, Chamberlain, without consulting the French, persuaded Hitler to sign a piece of paper declaring Britain and Germany's intention never to go to war with one another again. Hitler scarcely bothered to read it, but duly signed. Chamberlain returned to Britain in triumph proclaiming that he had brought back "peace in our time". Czechoslovakia was now a defenceless rump but was still an independent republic.

The peace had been saved, but the achievements of Munich were soon to prove illusory. The vulnerability of Czechoslovakia was underlined when Slovak separatists, demanding independence, appealed to Hitler for military assistance. On 15 March 1939, Hitler sent his army into Prague in clear violation of the Munich agreement and Czechoslovakia was finally dismembered. Bohemia and Moravia became a "Protectorate" of the Third Reich and placed under direct German rule; Slovakia became an independent state, and Hungary occupied the province of Ruthenia. Czechoslovakia had paid the supreme price for the democracies' attempts at trying to preserve peace in Europe. It was now almost inevitable that Hitler's next victim would be Poland.

Munich represented both the apotheosis, and the end, of appeasement. Far from securing "peace in our time", it culminated in a triumph for naked aggression. By the end of 1938, Hitler, not Chamberlain, dominated the diplomatic stage of Europe. Nevertheless, the butchering of Czechoslovakia marked a significant turning point in Britain's and France's diplomacy towards Germany. The events in Czechoslovakia had persuaded Chamberlain and Daladier that Hitler was bent on the domination of central and eastern Europe.

Both Britain and France used the year between Munich and the final outbreak of war to speed up their rearmament programme.

There has been much discussion about appeasement and what might have happened if Britain and France had decided to go to war with Germany in 1938. As with the First World War, the origins of the Second have sparked considerable controversy. In assessing Hitler's responsibility for the outbreak of war in 1939, considerable attention has been devoted to the so-called Hossbach Memorandum. This is a record of a secret meeting Hitler held towards the end of 1937 with his top military brass and his Foreign Minister in which he outlined the aims of German policy and the possible courses it might follow. These are not official minutes in a formal sense, rather an account that Friedrich Hossbach, Hitler's military adjutant, made from memory some five days later. The Hossbach Memorandum was used as a key prosecution document at the Nuremberg trials when it was cited as a timetable for German aggression. Although there is no serious reason to doubt its accuracy, it is, in fact, a copy of a copy – the original having disappeared.

Hitler began by asserting that the subject of the meeting was too important for a full cabinet meeting. The preservation of the racial community depended on "living space" and this could only be achieved by "the use of force" ("and this was never without attendant risk"). Germany, however, would only be fully prepared for war in the mid 1940s but could not afford to wait that long. If an opportunity presented itself before that date, it must be taken. In order to improve Germany's "politico-military situation", the first objective was the overthrowing of Czechoslovakia and Austria. Hossbach noted that the "Führer believed that almost certainly Britain, and probably France ... had tacitly written off the Czechs and were reconciled to the fact that this question would be cleared up in due course by Germany" (Welch 1994: 183–4). Hitler was also confident that Mussolini would not object to an *Anschluss* with Austria.

German foreign policy after 1937 bore a striking resemblance to the strategy minuted by Colonel Hossbach. If the Hossbach Memorandum was a premeditated masterplan for European domination, then whatever foreign policy the democracies adopted would have led to eventual conflict. Appeasement can be discounted as the root cause of war, as war would have been inevitable. Alternatively, it is possible to argue that Hitler was not planning war but setting out long-term aims and taking the opportunity outside a minuted cabinet meeting to think aloud and make warlike noises. By adopting a position of appeasement, Britain and France tempted Hitler to gamble further and to take bigger risks, convinced that they would remain passive. When Göring asked Hitler on the eve of war why it had been necessary to take such a huge gamble, he replied: "All my life I have gone for broke."

My own feeling is that the Hossbach Memorandum records Hitler attempting to win the support of his General Staff and Foreign Minister for acquiring living space in eastern Europe within a specified time limit, and by force if necessary. The sense of urgency that Hitler conveyed is in marked contrast to the anxiety expressed by Minister of War von Blomberg and Commander in Chief of the army Werner Fritsch and later by Neurath (Foreign Office) about the consequences of precipitate German military action. Within weeks of the meeting, the army had set out a strategic plan for an offensive against Czechoslovakia, and a few months later a bloodless purge removed the remnants of the conservative old guard (16 generals in all including Blomberg and Fritsch) who had failed to respond more positively to Hitler's plans. Although the significance of the meeting of 5 November is being reassessed by historians, it repre-sented a dramatic turning point that eventually led to Hitler assuming control of the armed forces and in the process emasculating the army as an independent force. Neurath was replaced at the Foreign Office by the arrogant and incompetent Joachim von Ribbentrop. (Göring referred to him as that "dirty little champagne peddlar", and Goebbels remarked: "He bought his name, he married his money, and he swindled his way into office.") Moreover, the economic conditions necessary to wage war that had initially been master-minded by Schacht (leading to serious shortages in manpower, raw materials and capital) were further radicalized by forcing the Ministry of Economics to set aside rational economic planning in the interests of increasing armament production. By mid 1938, Hitler had sufficiently weakened potential opposition from conservative elites and could now initiate an expansionist foreign policy in pursuit of German hegemony. On 10 November 1938, he summoned 400 of the regime's leading journalists to Munich and instructed them in their future role in the coming war:

> It is absolutely necessary gradually to prepare the German people psychologically for the coming war and to make it clear to them that there are some things which only force, not peaceful means, must decide. (Welch 1995: 89)

The German people, Hitler said, must be as strong as Krupp steel and stand united behind their Führer. Propaganda Minister Goebbels now switched track and claimed that war was unavoidable and was being forced upon Germany. Anticipating Germany's expansion as a major world power, propaganda set out to psychologically prepare and mobilize the nation into a "fighting community" for war. An ominous slogan of the period proclaimed "Today Germany, tomorrow, the World".

Following the invasion of Czechoslovakia in March 1939, Britain abandoned appeasement and on 31 March Chamberlain announced that Britain and France would guarantee Poland's independence. On 3 April the German General Staff was ordered to prepare for war against Poland. German grievances against Poland stemmed from the 1919 peace settlements and the loss of the Polish corridor, which now separated East Prussia from the rest of Germany, and the former German port of Danzig which was made an "open city" under the League's jurisdiction.

Soon after the announcement of the guarantee, the British and French started negotiations with the Soviet Union to try to establish a common front against Germany. However, long-standing Anglo-French mistrust of the motives of the Soviet Union, together with Poland's refusal in August to allow Russian troops on her territory in the event of a war between the Soviet Union and Germany, finally sank the negotiations. The Germans, on the other hand, keen to prevent such a *rapprochement*, stepped in and persuaded Stalin to sign a non-aggression pact on 23 August with secret clauses on the partition of Poland. The signing of the Nazi–Soviet Pact is, perhaps, one of the most controversial acts in the period leading up to war. Writing some years later in his memoirs, Nikita Khrushchev referred to the Soviet Union's motives in signing the pact:

> We knew perfectly well that Hitler was trying to trick us with the treaty. I heard with my own ears how Stalin said, "Of course it's all a game to see who can fool whom. I know what Hitler's

up to. He thinks he's outsmarted me, but actually it's I who have tricked him!" Stalin told Voroshilov, Beria, myself, and some other members of the Politbureau that because of this treaty the war would pass us by for a while longer. We would be able to stay neutral and save our strength. Then we would see what happened ... It was like a gambit in chess: if we hadn't made that move, the war should have started earlier, much to our disadvantage. As it was, we were given a respite ... For their part, the Germans too were using the treaty as a manoeuvre to win time. Their idea was to divide and conquer the nations which had united against Germany in World War I and which might unite against Germany again. Hitler wanted to deal with his adversaries one at a time. He was convinced that Germany had been defeated in World War I because she had tried to fight on two fronts at once. The treaty he signed with us was his way of trying to limit the coming war to one front. (Khrushchev 1971: 150–52)

At the time, the signing of the pact was widely viewed as a cynical reversal of ideological allegiances. It appeared to undermine the Anti-Comintern Pact and be at odds with Hitler's talk of a crusade against Bolshevism. Khrushchev's record confirms that the Soviets were under no illusions about Hitler's intentions and anticipated that "eventually we would be drawn into the war". According to Khrushchev, both sides viewed the treaty as an exercise in short-term pragmatic politics. Germany sought to avoid a war on two fronts and Stalin, having purged his High Command in 1937, used the treaty "as a manoeuvre to win time". More recently, a younger generation of Russian historians have dismissed the theory that Stalin sought to gain time to prepare his own defences, pointing to the fact that there is little evidence of these preparations actually taking place. Indeed, with the advance of the Soviet borders into Poland the old defences were dismantled but new ones were not constructed so as not to alarm Hitler. New research suggests, controversially, that the real basis for the pact was psychological and that Hitler was possibly the only man Stalin ever trusted. The orthodox explanation that Stalin was merely "playing for time" may well have been a retro-spective justification for his political naïvety (Sakwa, forthcoming). In a secret clause to the treaty, Germany and Russia agreed to establish spheres of influence in eastern central Europe with the immediate partition of Poland. Hitler fixed the date for his attack on Poland for 26 August.

On 22 August, the eve of the signing of the Nazi–Soviet Non-Aggression Pact, an exultant Hitler gathered the senior commanders of his armed forces to the Berghof and exhorted them to be resolute. Referring to himself as a "Man of Destiny" who held the question of war and peace in his hands, Hitler informed his generals that this was the most propitious time to act against Poland:

> All these fortunate circumstances will no longer prevail in two or three years. No one knows how long I shall live ... A beginning has been made with the destruction of England's hegemony. The way is open for the soldier, now that I have made the political preparations ... In starting and making war it is not right, but victory, that matters. Have no pity. Brutal attitude. Eighty million people must get what is their right. Their existence must be secured. Might is right. (quoted Bullock 1952: 482–3)

The elimination of France and Britain was a prerequisite for his expansion in the east and his ultimate intention to create *Lebensraum*. While Ribbentrop talked enthusiastically of German–Russian *rapprochement* there is no evidence to suggest that, with the signing of the Nazi–Soviet Non-Aggression Pact, Hitler had abandoned the ideas he had expressed in *Mein Kampf* and in the *Second book*. Hitler remained wedded to territorial conquest in the east to secure Germany's "living space". However, all the pieces of the jigsaw had to be in place before he could launch an attack on Russia. That included detaching the Western powers from their former ally in the east, thus protecting Hitler from having to fight a war on two fronts.

Hitler believed that the announcement of the non-aggression pact would demonstrate to the British and the French the futility of their promises to Poland. The pact paved the way for Hitler's attack on Poland, which von Ribbentrop had convinced him would not be opposed by Britain. Chamberlain, however, continued to back Poland, and on 25 August signed an Anglo-Polish mutual assistance treaty while still seeking to achieve a negotiated settlement. When Germany invaded Poland on 1 September, the British government issued an ultimatum to Germany which expired on 3 September. First

Britain and then France declared war on the same day and thus the Second World War began.

On 1 September Hitler addressed the Reichstag and somewhat uneasily defended the pact with Russia ("Germany has no intention of exporting its doctrine") and explained the Polish campaign as one of self-defence. Disclaiming any quarrel with Britain or France he said that Polish atrocities and border provocations had compelled him to answer force with force ("bombs will be met with bombs"). He ended his tortuous address with a melodramatic gesture by drawing attention to the mission that Providence had decreed for him:

> I am asking of no German man more than I myself was ready to do throughout four years. There will be no hardships for Germans to which I myself will not submit. My whole life belongs henceforth more than ever to my people. I am from now on just the first soldier of the German Reich....

He then pledged that he would not remove his field grey uniform until final victory – or he would not live to see its end. Almost as an aside Hitler informed the assembly that should anything happen to him, he had nominated Göring as his successor, demonstrating once again the arbitrary nature of Führer absolutism.

During the early days of September Hitler was haunted by the prospect of a war against England, which he affirmed might end in defeat. However, the remarkable success of the German armed forces in Poland militated against sombre reflections and recriminations. Aware that not all his generals were enthusiastic about extending the war by an attack in the west, Hitler penned a lengthy memorandum on 9 October for his Commanders-in-Chief and Halder and Keitel:

> The German war aim is a final military settlement with the West, that is, the destruction of the power and the ability of the Western Powers ever again to oppose the State Consolidation and further developments of the German people in Europe. As far as the outside world is concerned, this aim will have to undergo various propaganda adjustments, necessary from a pyschological point of view. This does not alter the war aim. That is and remains the destruction of our western enemies.

The repeated postponement of the invasion of Britain has recently prompted some historians to speculate (mistakenly, in my view) that Hitler never seriously intended to launch Operation Sealion. Hitler's eagerness to eliminate France and Britain at the earliest opportunity was predicated on Russia staying out of the conflict. However, Hitler never lost sight of his long-term objective – the struggle for *Lebensraum* in the east – nor his pathological distrust of his new ally. The memorandum continued:

> By no treaty or pact can a lasting neutrality of Soviet Russia be insured with safety. At present all reasons speak against Russia's departure from this state of neutrality. In eight months, one year or several years this may be altered. (quoted Bullock 1952: 518)

The offensive in the west which Hitler initially set for 12 November 1939 was repeatedly postponed. Furious at what he perceived to be the defeatism of the High Command, Hitler summoned his commanders to a conference on 23 November to hear him speak. He claimed that for the first time since Bismarck, Germany had no need to fear a war on two fronts. The pact with Russia had not secured Germany's future but it had bought time. He then seemed to be carried away by events and began talking about the "great men in history" theme that had dominated his thinking since writing *Mein Kampf* 15 years before:

> I have led the German people to a great height, even if the world does hate us now. I am setting this work on a gamble. I have to choose between victory and destruction. I choose victory. Greatest historical choice, to be compared with the decision of Frederick the Great before the First Silesian War. Prussia owes its rise to the heroism of one man. Even the closest advisers were disposed to capitulate. Everything depended on Frederick the Great ... The spirit of the great men of history must hearten us all ... As long as I live I shall think only of the victory of my people ... In the last years I have experienced many examples of intuition. Even in the present development I see prophecy. If we come through this struggle victoriously – and we shall – our time will enter into the history of our people. (quoted Bullock 1952: 521)

Clearly in an excited mood, Hitler finished prophetically: "I shall stand or fall in this struggle. I shall never survive the defeat of my people. No capitulation to the forces outside; no revolution from within."

Although this speech was intended to inspire his generals, not all were convinced. Walter von Brauchitsch, who had succeeded Fritsch as Commander-in-Chief of the Wehrmacht, tried unsuccessfully to offer his resignation after the meeting while other officers failed to share their Führer's eagerness for the conflict ahead. However, as Alan Bullock has stated, the vacillating doubts of the High Command would prove insufficient to halt Hitler in a mood which had been hardened into reckless determination by his victory in Poland. For his part, Hitler was now convinced of the historical parallel between himself and Frederick the Great. Convinced of Providence's intention "to allow me to reach my goal" he would no longer take advice from his generals on military matters, preferring instead to be guided by his own intuition. Hitler's megalomania was already evident as he began to embark on alarming flights from reality. Throughout his mono-logues, there are constant references to "Providence", to himself as a man of destiny, and to his life-long mission – all in the name of the German people who were expected to soar with him on his eagle's flight to the Walhallian heights – or die in the fall! Not surprisingly, many generals (including a cluster around Ludwig Beck) bitterly resented Hitler's meddling in military matters, fearing that it would eventually lead to defeat. However, these "vacillating" generals, constrained by their loyalty oath, continued to back their Führer even when their own military instincts dictated the reverse. Moreover, as Hitler's astonishing military success increased, the possibility of this group removing him became less and less.

Hitler's confidence in the superiority of the German army over the French proved well founded. Despite all his uncertainties in unleash-ing a war, Hitler was enjoying unparalleled popularity and prestige. The Italian Foreign Minister, Count Ciano, noted in his diary that at his meeting with the Führer on 1 October 1939, the hesitations which had beset him during the months before the attack on Poland were now replaced by a serene self-confidence (Ciano 1947: 162). Rapid and relatively bloodless victories in the west followed in 1940. Hitler was now at the pinnacle of his personal power and popularity. Poland was overrun in 19 days, Denmark and Norway in two months,

Holland, Belgium, Luxembourg and France in six weeks. Hitler's standing amongst the population reached its highest point with the signing of the armistice with France on 22 June 1940. The euphoria of Hitler's territorial expansion had even overshadowed the general discontent felt about coal shortages, the workings of the rationing system and the increasing regimentation of life within Germany. Had Hitler retired or died in June 1940 when only Britain stood firm, he would have been heralded as Germany's greatest statesman since Bismarck.

The victory over France marked the high point of Nazi propaganda but was to prove the last great military success the Germans would celebrate (although in the following April German troops were sent into Greece, Yugoslavia and then Egypt). Nevertheless, the special *Deutsche Wochenschau* (German film newsreel) of Hitler's "Triumphant Return to Berlin", released to celebrate the fall of France, testifies to the remarkable nature of the cult of the Führer. The train journey back to Germany from France, and particularly his arrival in Berlin, where he is greeted by the *Bund deutscher Mädel* (League of German Girls) and adoring women, is a powerful emotional reminder of the manner in which the Hitler myth was presented. The final scene culminates in Hitler receiving the ecstatic crowd's adulation from the balcony of the Reich Chancellery.

Intoxicated by the dazzling *Blitzkrieg* victories, Hitler was a loose cannon who refused to listen to the warnings of his military and economic advisers that in the long run the war could not be won. On 31 July 1940, at a meeting at Berchtesgaden, Hitler had ordered his military chiefs to prepare for an all-out attack on the Soviet Union. The attack was to take place in May 1941 and Russia was to be overrun within five months. Hitler was taking possibly the biggest gamble of his career. On 22 June 1941, having postponed indefinitely the invasion of Britain, Hitler launched Operation Barbarossa, the invasion of the Soviet Union. Although anticipating a similar victory in the east to that achieved by *Blitzkrieg* in the west, Hitler had underestimated Russia's resources and her resolve. This error of judgement was compounded by Germany's gratuitous declaration of war on the United States after Pearl Harbor had been bombed by the Japanese. What had started as a European conflict was now a world war. By the beginning of 1942 Hitler had begun to lose control of the military situation. Despite hopelessly premature announcements of an early victory in the east, the Russians held Moscow, the Americans had now entered the conflict and, now that he had committed the fundamental error of waging war on two fronts, Hitler's short-comings as a strategist were exposed. Hitler no longer determined the course and character of events. Fascism was everywhere in retreat, but its total destruction would require two extra-European powers – the USA and the USSR – to occupy the imperial capital of Berlin, thus radically transforming the balance of power in Europe.

Though it meant resurrecting the German nightmare of a war on two fronts, Hitler rationalized his decision to attack the Soviet Union (perhaps the most important decision of his career) by arguing that it would prevent Britain from continuing the war with any prospect of success. Ian Kershaw is technically correct in suggesting that strategic and economic factors played a more important role than Hitler's ideological obsessions in the actual framing of the decision to attack (Kershaw 1991: 153). Nevertheless once it had been formulated by Hitler, the war against Russia (unlike the war in the west) was to be an anti-Bolshevik crusade, a war of annihilation in which the fate of European Jewry would finally be sealed. In his famous speech to the Reichstag on 30 January 1939 Hitler had prophesied that

If the international Jewish financiers outside Europe should succeed in plunging the nations once more into war, then the result will not be the Bolshevization of the earth, and thereby the victory of Jewry, but the annihilation of the Jewish race in Europe! (quoted Welch 1983: 299)

Christopher Browning has chillingly reminded us that the "quantum leap" into genocide was taken in the spring of 1941 when the planning of the invasion of Russia began to be worked out in detail. By the late summer of 1941, the dynamics of the campaign in the east meant that war and the fate of the Jews became inexorably linked. (This will be discussed in the next chapter.)

The controversies over the polycratic nature of Hitler's leadership extend also to his foreign policy. Most historians would agree that Hitler was much more interested in foreign affairs than he was in domestic policy. Was he the driving force behind German foreign policy or an arbiter between competing groups such as the army, the Foreign Office, the Party and big business? There are two long-standing interpretations. The first is that Hitler was an ideological "visionary" with a programme for territorial expansion and that these ideological fixations shaped German foreign policy. The other view suggests that he was not governed by an ideological blueprint, but he was a supreme opportunist. These two views are not mutually exclusive nor necessarily contradictory. It is possible to argue that Hitler did have fixed views on the nature of territorial expansion that always included colonizing Russia for *Lebensraum*. On the other hand he was ruthless enough to exploit the opportunites which were presented to him in foreign affairs – not least of which was the western democracies' policy of appeasement. It is possible therefore to synthesize the "intentionalist" and "structuralist" arguments and suggest that German foreign policy during the Third Reich was shaped by a combination of ideology, opportunity, and the weaknesses of the western democracies. These factors reinforced each other and generated a momentum of their own so that within the theatre of diplomacy and war Hitler was the leading player – but not always the director. As both a gambler and an opportunist Hitler never lost sight of his long-term objective, but there was no timetable or blueprint for aggression.

Martin Broszat, for example, sees little evidence of shape and design in Hitler's foreign policy. There were confusions and contradictions in the manner in which Hitler conducted his foreign policy. For example the pact with Russia in 1939 flew in the face of Hitler's own worldview that history was a racial struggle against Judaism and its political manifestation, Marxism. On the other hand, there is Hitler's well-known comment to Carl Burckhardt, the Swiss Commissioner to the League of Nations, in 1939:

> Everything that I undertake is directed against Russia. If those in the West are too stupid and too blind to understand this, then I shall be forced to come to an understanding with the Russians to beat the West, and then, after its defeat, turn with all my concerted force against the Soviet Union. (Hildebrand 1973: 88)

While it is possible to argue that Hitler's foreign policy lacked consistency and design, it is difficult to conceive of Nazi policy without Hitler being the prime mover in the decision-making process. The broad lines of policy were determined by Hitler himself. Some of the most momentous decisions made in the Third Reich, such as the crucial decision to repeatedly postpone the invasion of Britain, Operation Barbarossa, and the declaration of war against the USA, were made by Hitler and no-one else – and in the face of conventional military wisdom. I cannot think of one example of Nazi foreign policy that was shaped without Hitler's distinctive imprint. When Hitler wanted something he invariably got his way. Ribbentrop occasionally was allowed to offer advice and individual generals attempted to apply the brakes to Hitler's headlong rush into war, but, having assumed personal control of all military operations, and convinced that he was guided by Providence and that conditions were favourable to Germany, Hitler refused to listen. Warnings were dismissed as defeatism. The relationship between Hitler and the army is a complex one; arguably this traditionally conservative elite remained the only group capable of removing Hitler. How did army officers respond to Hitler's irrational leadership at times of mounting crises? A brave few decided to resist in July 1944 and plotted unsuccessfully to remove Hitler. He, in turn, pursued those implicated in the assassination attempt with relentless determination. Evidence from recent research, notably from a volume of essays edited by Salewski and Schulze-Wegener, suggests that many officers who could not oppose Hitler (because of their oath of loyalty) instead applied creative thinking to circumvent the obstacles posed by Hitler's impossible orders. In so doing they may well have prolonged the war and the life of the Third Reich (Salewski & Schulze-Wegener 1995).

War was not accidental to Hitler; it was at the very core of his worldview. Hitler's attempt to overcome what he viewed as the disadvantages of Germany's traditional position as a central European power ("*Mittelmachtfatalitäten*") by means of armed conflict and racial warfare (*Rassenkrieg*) led inexorably to territorial expansion and conflict. Hitler had written in *Mein Kampf* and in the *Second book* that the world was locked in a permanent struggle in which the stronger must prevail. Germany needed to expand and like the British required colonies. This historical "vision" did not necessarily represent a radical departure from the views of former German Chancellors. Indeed, in 1938, with the successful *Anschluss* of Austria, Hitler had achieved something beyond his predeccessors, namely the dream of "*Grossdeutschland*" ("Greater Germany"). But there the path linking Bismarck with Hitler ends (if it ever began). Hitler saw the Greater German Reich merely as one stage towards the headlong rush into the Greater *Germanic* Reich. To fulfil this far more ambitious vision he looked eastwards for territorial expansion, to create a racist empire at the expense of the Slav *Untermenschen* (sub-humans). His aims were to control, colonize, and exploit the Slavic population whom he viewed as fit only for slavery:

> The Slavs are a mass of born slaves, who feel the need of a master ... Our role in Russia will be analogous to that of England in India ... To-day everybody is dreaming of a world peace conference. For my part, I prefer to wage war for another ten years rather than be cheated thus of the spoils of victory ... The German people will raise itself to the level of this empire. (*Hitler's table talk*, 17 September 1941)

Hitler was convinced that once the racial-ideological war against Russia had been launched, as he told Jodl, "the whole rotten edifice of [communist rule] [would] come tumbling down" and the campaign would be over in six weeks.

Writing some years ago, Tim Mason argued that the strains imposed on the German economy by attempting to provide both "guns and butter" had led to an economic crisis in 1939 which in turn was one factor persuading Hitler to start a war as a way out of the situation (Mason 1972). However, recent research on Nazi foreign policy has confirmed that Hitler was no weak dictator with limited ambitions who was pushed into war by economic crisis in 1939 against his own choosing. According to Richard Overy, whose distinguished work on the Nazi economy and war has challenged many of the accepted views of economic policy under Hitler, "From the point of view of German military and economic preparations, the war that broke out in the autumn of 1939 was the wrong war" (Overy 1994: 203). This returns me to the question I posed in the opening paragraph of this chapter. The events that unfolded in 1939 were not of Hitler's choosing, although he must bear the major responsibility. In terms of his doctrinaire beliefs he was, indeed, fighting the "wrong war". But it was a gamble that Hitler was prepared to risk knowing that the momentum of his expansionist drive inevitably led to war with the Soviet Union. In order to prevent (or at least delay)

America's entry into the conflict and force Britain to the conference table, the Soviet Union would have to be destroyed within a matter of months. Overy argues that Hitler promoted intense rearmament, not for *Blitzkrieg*, but for this more ambitious large-scale war. Overy's conclusions are largely supported by the works of Gerhard Weinberg who, in a long and productive career, has consistently maintained that Hitler's doctrinaire convictions decisively shaped Nazi foreign policy. Dealing with the Danzig question in early 1939, Weinberg contends that already on principle Hitler was choosing war as a preferred means for solving international disagreements. Hitler's reaction to the Japanese attack on Pearl Harbor is cited as further evidence of a pre-existing, ideologically based desire to seek out war against the USA sooner or later (Weinberg 1995). Interestingly enough, when writing in 1928 in his *Second book*, Hitler paid tribute to America in racial terms, as a country that "felt itself to be a Nordic-German state and in no way an international mishmash of peoples" (Hitler 1961: 108). Hitler believed that the rising power of the USA would compel Britain to seek an alliance with Germany. His views changed dramatically after Pearl Harbor when he declared feelings of "hatred and deep repugnance" for all things American. Describing America as being "half Judaised and the other half negrified" he dismissed the USA as a "decayed country" without "much future" (*Hitler's table talk*, 7 January 1942).

The fundamental conception of Hitler's foreign policy was flawed from the start. Not only was Germany unprepared for an ambitiously expansionist war in 1939 as a result of structural defects of the regime, but, as Peter Hayes has pointed out, Nazi foreign policy in 1939 was bound to arouse a hostile coalition of great powers whose resources would inevitably outstretch those of the Third Reich (Hayes 1987). Obsessed by unlimited territorial expansion in the east that would provide "space" for the creation of a master race and supported by economic autarky (*Grossraumwirtschaft*), Hitler's grandiose vision of a Greater Germanic Reich could only be achieved by means of force. It represented a gamble unparalleled in recent European history. Moreover, his vision had been built on shaky economic and financial foundations. Hitler was not interested in the means that had enabled Germany to rearm. It had fallen to Schacht to finance Germany's rearmament programme by a sophisticated system of loans (the so-called "Mefo" bills) that effectively mortgaged Germany's future in the hope that rapid military conquest would provide raw materials and cheap labour.

From the outset Hitler was a "racial revolutionary" whose "utopian vision" was inexorably bound up with his desire to "solve" the "Jewish Question". The widening of the conflict into a world war by the end of 1941 finally persuaded Hitler to implement the "Final Solution to the Jewish Question" which had been under consideration since 1939. To understand Hitler's decision to wage war on two fronts in 1941, one must recognize the all-embracing importance of the other major plank in his *Weltanschauung*, namely his anti-Semitism. Territorial expansion and "removal of the Jews", two central features of Hitler's worldview, are examples of what Ian Kershaw has referred to as "the shift from utopian 'vision' to practical policy options taking shape". Kershaw maintains that by 1938 the two had come together in "sharp focus". Indeed he goes further and controversially suggests that a symbiotic relationship can be traced between the structural disorder of the Nazi state and the radicalization of policy implemented in its name (Kershaw 1993: 113). In other words, as the war progressed and Nazi rule disintegrated into further chaos, individuals and groups operating with the "will of the Führer" implemented "initiatives" that culminated in barbaric programmes of destruction and horror. The evolution of Hitler's anti-Semitic policy is discussed in the next chapter.

The translation into policy of Hitler's grandiose fixation for territorial expansion resulted in the Second World War and untold misery for millions. It also brought about an end to the Third Reich and to Hitler. He spoke of himself as a man called by Providence to restore Germany to greatness, but he chose not to survive the defeat of his people and committed suicide in the bunker of the Reich Chancellery on 30 April 1945.

Hitler (*right*) as a frontline soldier. Seen here with fellow dispatch messengers Ernst Schmidt and Anton Bachmann and his dog 'Foxl' at Fournes, April 1915. (© Bildarchiv Preussischer Kulturbesitz, Berlin)

Hitler as 'Führer'. Phographed by Heinrich Hoffmann in 1926 surrounded by his followers and looking every bit the 'man of destiny'. (© Bildarchiv Preussischer Kulturbesitz, Berlin)

Hitler's charisma. A 1932 election poster of his disembodied head against a
black background. (Supplied by The Weiner Library, London)

Hitler with President Hindenburg shortly after Hitler became Chancellor in 1933. A rare picture of Hitler smiling. (AKG, London)

The popular leader in 1933 receiving flowers from a child. Himmler can be seen in the background. (© Bildarchiv Preussischer Kulturbesitz, Berlin)

Hitler justifying the 'Night of the Long Knives' and the purging of the SA to the Reichstag, 13 July 1934. (© Bildarchiv Preussischer Kulturbesitz, Berlin)

Hitler and Himmler at the 1938 Nazi Party Congress. (© Bildarchiv
Preussischer Kulturbesitz, Berlin)

One of a series of statesmanlike portraits taken by Heinrich Hoffmann in 1938 when Hitler was 49 years old. (© Bildarchiv Preussischer Kulturbesitz, Berlin)

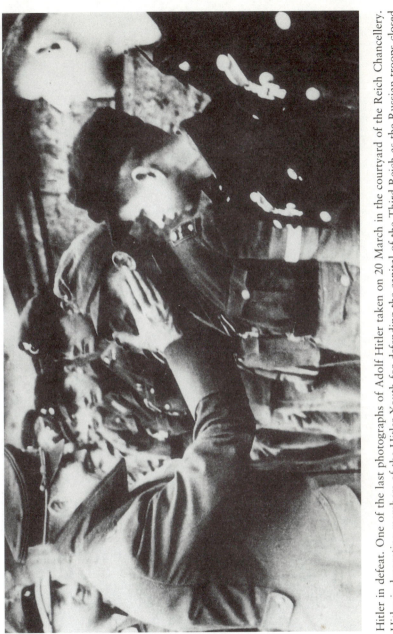

Hitler in defeat. One of the last photographs of Adolf Hitler taken on 20 March in the courtyard of the Reich Chancellery. Hitler is decorating members of the Hitler Youth for defending the capital of the Third Reich as the Russian troops closed around Berlin. (Becker Collection/Weiner Library)

CHAPTER FIVE

Hitler and the Holocaust

Why did the Third Reich launch a war of genocide that resulted in destruction on a hitherto unprecedented scale and what precisely was Hitler's role in all this? "Intentionalists" such as Klaus Hildebrand and Karl Dietrich Bracher concluded that Nazi leaders, above all Hitler, did so because they wanted to. The ultimate goal of Nazism was genocide and as such the Third Reich stands out as a unique epoch (an "accidental aberration") in Germany's otherwise proud and healthy history. By tracing the worst atrocities that occurred in the years 1938–45 to Hitler's *Weltanschauung* they believed they could demonstrate a causal explanation. For "intentionalist" historians, Hitler was a "programmatist" consistently pursuing defined ideological objectives. Historians like Hildebrand have maintained that the mass murder of the Jews was the culmination of Hitler's pathological ideology: "Fundamental to National Socialist genocide was Hitler's race dogma" (Hildebrand 1984: 178). Hildebrand even suggested that we should refer to "Hitlerism" rather than "National Socialism". While accepting that the Third Reich was a chaotic form of government, scholars such as Hildebrand nevertheless claim that this very chaos enhanced Hitler's authority and, by implication, the moral responsibility for the Holocaust.

More recently "structuralists" have been engaged in a fundamental review of this position. The result has been to downgrade the position of Hitler and reconnect Nazism to the German past by emphasizing the importance of traditional elites in governing the Third Reich. Such historians concentrate on the *structural* context of political decision-making. Hans Mommsen, for example, has coined the phrase "cumulative radicalization" to suggest that the forces unleashed by the Nazis when they took over power led to a spiral of increasingly radical and often irreconcilable policies. "Structuralists" argue that the Nazi leadership viewed the administrative structure of the state as a burdensome limitation on their power. Propaganda and evasion were frequently substituted for policy and administration. *Ad hoc* agencies which invariably became permanent were established to deal with specific problems, with the result that decision-making became fragmented, conflicts sharpened and co-ordinating policy became virtually impossible. Individuals or departments might press for a radicalization of policy in ideologically important areas not simply as a consequence of intrinsic ideologically determined priorities but as part of a wider attempt to assert their authority over rival individuals or groups. In the case of the "Final Solution", for example, this involved ruthless killing units competing with each other to exceed murder quotas handed down to them by anonymous bureaucrats. These actions would not only secure personal advancement but, equally importantly, they demonstrated to superiors ideological commitment to the Führer's goals. In such a highly competitive and chaotic cauldron decisions, taken in a vacuum, assumed a momentum of their own. The unanticipated consequences of these often required even more far-reaching and radical solutions. In this structural context, whereby all decisions had to reflect "the will of the Führer", Hitler's power was notably enhanced, although he was not necessarily able (or willing) to keep this cumulative effect in check. To some extent Hitler became a prisoner of the chaos that he had helped to unleash; in order to maintain his popularity he began to dissociate himself from the more unpopular policies and decisions, while at the same time encouraging the more radical policies of his subordinates even if such policies clashed with each other. According to Mommsen, once this "cumulative radicalization" was unleashed the process became self-generating and ultimately self-destructive. It also circumscribed Hitler's scope, hence Mommsen's famous claim that Hitler was a "weak dictator". In other words, Hitler may have benefited from the chaos he had created but he was not necessarily consciously shaping policy nor in complete control of the dynamics he had unleashed.

Hans Mommsen downplays Hitler as a causative force of cumulative radicalization: "it is a serious mistake to concentrate study of Nazi tyranny on the analysis of the role which Hitler occupied in it" (Mommsen 1991: 187). As with so many issues in the Third Reich, the reappraisal by "structuralist" historians like Mommsen (and particularly Martin Broszat) provided a sophisticated analytical framework within which to analyze Hitler and Nazism and in so doing they have deepened our understanding of the complexities involved. In the light of such research and in particular the notion of a "dysfunctional" Nazi state, it is difficult to argue that Hitler's likes and dislikes were always translated into policy decisions. Norman Rich's blanket "Hitler was master in the Third Reich" (Rich vol. 1 (1973): 11) is too simplistic. But equally it would be absurd to suggest, in the case of "cumulative radicalization", that Hitler's role can be ignored or downgraded.

There is no reason why Mommsen's notion of "cumulative radicalization" operating within a chaotic "structureless system" should necessarily downgrade Hitler's role in this process. In fact it is perfectly possible to embrace this model of analysis and to place Hitler squarely within such a framework, so that he becomes a key player in the "system". "Structurelessness" – or "administrative chaos" – provided the framework within which Hitler's "utopian visions" could be translated into policy. The territorial expansion outlined in Chapter 4 and Nazi Jewish policy – both central features of Hitler's *Weltanschauung* – had by 1939 come into the foreground as feasible policy options. In following years they would escalate into genocidal war. It is first necessary, however, to outline briefly the path that led to genocide before analyzing Hitler's role in its genesis.

Intrinsic to the idea of a "national community" was the Nazi belief in the need for racial purity, an issue dominated by the "Jewish Question" but one that really encompassed two main enemies: the threat posed by the Jew from within Germany, and the danger of the Slav *Untermenschen* ("sub-human Slavs") in Poland and Russia. As we have seen from Chapter 1, the underlying drive behind Hitler's racial teaching was the obsessive desire to bring Germans to a common awareness of their ethnic and political unity. Nazi racial teaching within the educational system, and propaganda in general, preached hatred of Jews and Slavs and proclaimed the superiority of the so-called Aryan race. The desire for racial purity centred on two interrelated themes; one was *Blut und Boden* ("blood and soil"), and the other was *Volk und Heimat* ("a people and a homeland"). The concept of "a people and a homeland" sprang directly from the doctrine of *Blut und Boden*, which attempted to define the source of strength of the *Herrenvolk* (master race) in terms of peasant virtues, the Nordic past, the warrior hero, and the sacredness of German soil, the last of which could not be confined by artificial boundaries imposed arbitrarily by a treaty such as Versailles.

Only a few months after coming to power, Hitler set about justifying the eradication of "inferior" human beings. The first people to be exterminated were not Jews but "unhealthy" Germans. On 14 July 1933, the new government approved the "Law for the Prevention of Hereditarily Diseased Offspring" which permitted the compulsory sterilization of people suffering from a number of allegedly "hereditary" illnesses. In order not to jeopardize the successful conclusion of the Concordat with the Holy See, the publication of the decree was delayed until 25 July. Although in theory this measure was discretionary, in practice it was compulsory. It came into effect on 1 January 1934; sterilization was required in cases of hereditary imbecility, schizophrenia, hereditary deafness, hereditary epilepsy, manic depression, Huntington's chorea, chronic alcoholism, and extreme physical malformation. During 1934, 32,268 sterilizations were carried out; the following year the figure increased to 73,174, and in 1936 63,547 people were sterilized. In 1935, the German bishops initially ruled that since the main purpose of marriage was procreation, sterilized persons could no longer partake of the sacrament of matrimony. However, the decision was swiftly reversed when it became clear that Catholic officials had helped enforce the law and that such a decision might alienate the growing number of Catholics who had actually been sterilized. Individual priests who protested against the sterilization law incurred immediate penalties and the regime responded by proclaiming that it was no longer prepared to tolerate any further sabotage of the law.

Given Hitler's' obsession with health and hygiene, it should come as no surprise to discover the existence of Nazi eugenics policies. Indeed, eugenic legislation was a logical outcome of National Socialist thought and propaganda which had always stressed the importance of achieving a pure and healthy race. At the Nuremberg Party rally in 1929 Hitler had cited ancient Sparta's policy of selective infanticide as a model for Nazi Germany: "If every year Germany had one million children and eliminated 700,000–800,000 of the weakest, the end result would probably be an increase in national strength" (quoted Lewy 1964: 258). Although Hitler's intentions were a matter of public record, he was never able to implement these ideas despite setting out the legislative machinery for such an operation should the occasion arise.

However, anti-Semitism was at the core of Hitler's ideology, and the Jewish stereotype that developed from it provided the focal point for the feeling of aggression inherent in the ideology. Before 1939, anti-Semitism was largely uncoordinated and propagated chiefly by means of the educational system and the press. Three major campaigns were waged, in 1933, 1935 and 1938. Immediately after the Nazi electoral victory in March 1933, rank-and-file Party activists went on the rampage assaulting Jews and damaging Jewish shops and demanding a "Jewish-free" economy. Hitler remained in the background while intimidation of Jews continued unchecked – although his long-standing anti-Semitism never wavered. He continued to view Jews as harbingers of "crime, corruption and chaos". They also posed a danger. In *Mein Kampf* he referred to Jews as a "noxious bacillus" that had to be removed from German blood and soil:

Bearing in mind the devastations which Jewish bastardisation visits on our nation each day, and considering that this blood poisoning can be removed from our national body only after centuries, if at all ... This contamination of our blood, blindly ignored by hundreds of thousands of our people, is carried on systematically by the Jew today. (Hitler 1939: 512)

It is one thing to have anti-Semitic prejudices, quite another to be able to implement such beliefs . Did Hitler conclude that he could "realize the unthinkable" and exterminate the Jews or did the "final solution" emerge gradually as a series of *ad hoc* pragmatic responses to changing political, economic and military circumstances?

The first few years of Nazi rule are characterized by persecution and intimidation of the Jews. Hitler did nothing to discourage this, although during a transitional stage for his government he remained sensitive to international opinion. Remember also he was engaged in other controversial actions such as suspending civil liberties and destroying the radical SA leadership under Ernst Röhm in the Blood Purge of 30 June 1934. Despite continued harassment at a local level there were no further official moves against Jews until September 1935 when, at the Party rally in Nuremberg, Hitler announced a further batch of anti-Jewish legislation.

Hitler had been under pressure for some time from Party activists to introduce more draconian measures. The Nuremberg Laws were divided into two sections and the ordinances (supplementary decrees) based on them followed in November 1935. The Reich Citizenship Law denied Jews the right of citizenship, the right to vote and to hold public office. In effect, Jews had been named *personae non gratae*. Interestingly enough, there appears to be a compromise over the classification of a Jew. The ordinance to the Citizenship Law states (article II,2) that those of mixed blood, i.e. with one or two non-Jewish grandparents, were entitled to German citizenship, albeit with certain restrictions. This represented a minor victory for "moderates" within the Interior Ministry who had successfully resisted attempts to restrict classification to one Jewish grandparent. The Law for the Protection of German Blood and Honour outlawed marriage between Jews and Gentiles and forbade sexual relations between them outside marriage. The law, which also denied Jews the right to fly the German flag, provided wide scope for the legal interpretation of "miscegenation" and laid Jews open to denunciation and framing. The fascination of many anti-Semites, including Hitler, with the sexual aspect of the legislation was an important feature of Nazi and anti-Semitic propaganda and found its most pornographic expression in Julius Streicher's semi-official broadsheet *Der Stürmer*, which specialized in denunciations of alleged Jewish immoral and sexual practices. The preamble to the law referred to the Reichstag "unanimously" adopting the legislation. Hitler obviously felt confident enough by September 1935 to pass such a racist law. Hindenburg, who had earlier emasculated attempts to prevent Jews from working in the civil service, was now dead, and the SA, who might have demanded even more radical measures, had been culled in the "Night of the Long Knives".

By the late 1930s the increasingly fanatical tone of propaganda reflected the growing radicalization of the regime's anti-Semitic policies. The *Anschluss* (union) with Austria in March 1938 served to accelerate the unlawful seizure of Jewish property. The position of German Jews deteriorated further still with the *Reichskristallnacht* (Night of the Broken Glass) of 9–10 November 1938, when Party activists unleashed by Goebbels and the Propaganda Ministry burned down synagogues and vandalized thousands of Jewish shops. This represented the most violent expression of anti-Jewish sentiment prior to the war and was named after the glass from the shattered windows of Jewish premises which littered the streets on the morning of 10 November 1938. On 9 November 1938 Ernst vom Rath, third secretary of the German Embassy in Paris, died having been shot two days earlier by a 17–year-old Polish Jew, Herschel Grynszpan. The boy was acting out of revenge for the forcible deportation from Germany of his parents. With thousands of others, they had been dumped across the Polish border during the previous month.

Although Jews had, for some time, been experiencing increased forms of discrimination and sporadic violence, the *Kristallnacht* did not come about as a result of long-term planning. The events of 9 November were seized upon by Propaganda Minister Goebbels, who was anxious to win back Hitler's favour after falling from grace because of an affair with the Czech actress, Lida Baarova. Goebbels used the opportunity of an "old fighters'" reunion in commemoration of the Munich *Putsch* of 9 November 1923, attended by Hitler, to propose a co-ordinated campaign of terror against Jews. We now know that the *Kristallnacht* was instigated by Goebbels but with Hitler's express approval. Groups of Party activists and storm-troopers were told to collect incendiary material to burn down their local synagogues and the police were ordered not to intervene. According to Nazi figures over 800 shops were destroyed, 191 synagogues set on fire and 76 synagogues demolished; 91 Jews were killed, 20,000 arrested and taken to concentration camps. The total damage to property was estimated at 25 million marks.

The pogrom was not in fact popular with large sections of the German people, who objected to the lawlessness, vandalism and destruction of property involved. Nevertheless, *Kristallnacht* marked a radicalization of Jewish policy with the aim of driving Jews out of German economic life altogether. To add insult to injury, they were required to meet the cost of the damage to their property themselves and on 12 November 1938 the Jewish community was ordered to pay a fine of 1 billion Reichmarks and excluded from German economic life, thus formalizing the "Aryanization" of Jewish-owned property which had begun in the autumn of 1937. The long-term significance of *Kristallnacht* was to convince the Nazi leadership of the limitations of an uncoordinated Jewish policy. In future, the "solution" to the so-called "Jewish problem" would be a more "rational" course of action carried out by the SS and with the public largely excluded. *Kristallnacht* represents a crucial junction on the road to Auschwitz.

The radicalization of German foreign policy had led to the invasion of the Soviet Union. As we have seen in Chapter 4, Operation Barbarossa was a war of extermination. With the entry of the USA into the war in December 1941 Hitler's huge military gamble was effectively lost. But Hitler was also engaged in another war – the systematic genocide of the Jews. This aimed at more than the population in Poland and Russia and involved nothing less than the Jewish population of Europe, estimated by the SS at approximately 10.5 million. Although the logistics of extermination would be delegated to the SS, locating Hitler's precise role in the "cumulative radicalization" of anti-Jewish policy is both complex and crucial. At one level this embraces the question of a so-called "Hitler order", and its corollary, the degree of complicity of the German population in the "Final Solution". The notion of "collective guilt" and the argument that the German people were Hitler's "willing executioners" has been given an added poignancy in recent years with the publication of Daniel Goldhagen's controversial and flawed best-seller (Goldhagen 1996).

Many historians agree that the "Final Solution of the Jewish Question" began with the German invasion of the Soviet Union on 22 June 1941. Ever since he wrote *Mein Kampf* Hitler continued to insist that the Jews were behind communism. The war with the Soviet Union provided him with an opportunity to crush both. Before Operation Bararossa was launched, it became an accepted principle of policy, which was explicitly approved by Hitler, that 30 million people in the occupied Soviet Union would be allowed to starve so that more food would be available for the German population and army (Housden 2000: 137, Gerlach 1998: 266ff.). Within a few months of the attack, what had been hitherto a hesitant and improvised campaign of mass murder was placed even more firmly under the central control of the SS, directed by Heinrich Himmler and his deputy Reinhard Heydrich. (The SS had had control of the Jewish Question since January 1939.) The growing involvement of the SS represents the connection between bureaucratic organization and charismatic leadership that was discussed in Chapter 3. The architect of the genocide, Heinrich Himmler, who had set up the first concentration camp in Dachau in 1933, had been outraged at the shambles of *Kristallnacht*. This former poultry farmer had proved himself to be a fanatical disciple of Hitler's race theory and, moreover, deferential to Hitler's will. In October 1939 Hitler appointed him Reich Commissar for the Strengthening of German Racial Identity (*Reichskommissar für die Festigung des Deutschen Volkstums*) and he was given absolute control over the newly annexed part of Poland. In the same year Reinhard Heydrich was appointed head of the Reich's Security Head Office (RSHA) which incorporated the Gestapo, the criminal police and the Security Service (SD). Between them, these two men rapidly accumulated enormous power together with the necessary administrative apparatus, manpower and technology to co-ordinate and implement the systematic extermination of European Jewry.

Four months after the invasion of the Soviet Union in October 1941, Heydrich, assisted by Adolf Eichmann, organized the mass deportation of Jews from Germany and Austria and annexed parts of Poland to the *General-Gouvernement*. The removal of Jews from the annexed parts of Poland was intended to make way for ethnic Germans, mainly from the Baltic. However, this created huge ghettos in areas like Kodz and Warsaw and it soon became clear that because of the numbers involved the strategy could not succeed. The lack of an overall plan of extermination at this stage is highlighted by the fact that sections of the SS were considering a bizarre Foreign Office proposal to ship European Jews to Madagascar in the Indian Ocean (although not necessarily for resettlement). On 31 July 1941, following the attack on the USSR, Heydrich had been given responsibility by Göring for carrying out the "total solution of the Jewish question in those territories of Europe which are under German influence" – with Himmler as the supreme overseer. Interestingly, the document charging him with taking on these responsibilities refers to both "total" solution (*Gesamtlösung*) and "final" solution (*Endlösung*). Equally revealing, both Göring's order – and Himmler in his speeches to his SS commanders – refer to fulfilling the 'Führer's wish' (Stargardt 1997: 346). By this stage *Einsatzgruppen* (specially selected SS units), with the co-operation of the Wehrmacht, were shooting Jews in the Soviet Union. In Germany, Party activists were demanding to have Jews from the Reich deported. With the ghettos bursting at the seams it was decided in the late summer of 1941 that mass extermination by poison gas was the solution. In December 1941 the first killing installations using mobile "gas vans" were operating at Chelmno in the Warthegau (a part of western Poland annexed to the

Reich). However, the "final solution" to the "Jewish question" was not implemented until after the Wannsee Conference of 20 January 1942 (which had been originally scheduled for 9 December 1941) finally co-ordinated measures for mass extermination. The conference had been convened by Reinhard Heydrich and appropriately enough given the circumlocutory language used to disguise mass murder (the "Final Solution" being another euphemism), the code-word used was "Operation Reinhard". By the end of March 1942 the mass extermination of Poland's Jewish population was under way in camps like Belzec, Sobibor and Treblinka. The most notorious extermination camp of all, Auschwitz-Birkenau, began its systematic mass gassings of Jews in June 1942. The process of "cumulative radicalization" which started with intimidation and persecution culminated in a network of extermination camps (all outside Germany in occupied Poland) and the slaughter of six million Jews (and over a quarter of a million Gypsies) during the Second World War. Similarly, Hitler's obsessive anti-Bolshevism culminating in his "war of annihilation" led to some three million Russian POWs dying – mostly of disease and starvation.

Is it possible that the implementation of mass extermination on a European scale could have been undertaken without the knowledge or approval of Hitler? Hitler's precise role in the Holocaust continues to divide historians. Interpretations are invariably shaped by the fundamental differences that exist over the nature of the Nazi state. This brings us back to the "Hitlerist" or "intentionalist" explanations versus the "structuralist" or "functionalist" ones. Was it a monolithic structure subservient to the all-embracing will of Hitler – or was it a shapeless and fragmented collection of competing individuals and institutions that included Hitler? The debate centres less on Hitler's knowledge and responsibility – few historians would absolve Hitler from complicity – than on whether or not Hitler had a clear plan and timetable for extermination. Furthermore, did Hitler personally order the "final solution"?

The guidelines for the war of extermination had been laid down by Hitler prior to the invasion of the Soviet Union. On 6 June 1941 in what has become known as the Commissar Order (*Kommissarbefehl*), Hitler instructed his generals that Red Army political commissars were to be shot without further ado. Prior to the outbreak of war Hitler had also been associated with the so-called euthanasia campaign. On 1 September 1939, the day that Poland was invaded, Hitler issued an order to kill all persons with incurable diseases. The idea of compulsory "euthanasia" had been in Hitler's mind for some time, but he had held back because of expected objections from the Catholic Church. The start of the war seemed the most propitious moment for inaugurating this radical eugenic programme. (The order was actually issued in October but backdated to 1 September.) After the war, at the Nuremberg doctors' trial, Dr Karl Brandt, the Reichs-kommissar for Health, testified that "In 1935 Hitler told the Reich Medical Leader, Dr Gerhard Wagner, that, if war came, he would take up and carry out this question of euthanasia because it was easier to do so in wartime when the church would not be able to put up the expected resistance" (quoted Reitlinger 1953: 125–6). Such a pro-gramme would also provide much-needed hospital space for the wounded. Thus the euthanasia programme was in direct line of suc-cession from the sterilization measures enacted in the early months of the regime.

Interestingly enough, as in the summer of 1941, so in the autumn of 1939, centrally organized and systematic killing was preceded by local initiatives. Between 29 September and 1 November 1939, SS units shot about 4,000 mental patients in asylums in Poland. The first "euthan-asia" installations opened in late December 1939 and early January 1940. As the so-called euthanasia action expanded, gassing in rooms designed as showers was introduced or lethal injections administered. It is estimated that between December 1939 and August 1941 at least 72,000 perished in institutions which operated under such fictitious names as "The Charitable Foundation for the Transportation of the Sick" and the "Charitable Foundation for Institutional Care".

Although corporately neither the churches nor the legal profession protested, individual clergy and lawyers did. Most notably, Bishop Galen of Münster, in a sermon delivered on 3 August 1941, revealed how the innocent sick were being killed while their families were misled by false death notices. The next of kin were notified that the patients had died of some ordinary disease and that their bodies had been cremated. Often they received warnings from the Secret Police not to demand explanations and not to "spread false rumours". Galen branded these deeds as criminal and demanded the prosecution for murder of those perpetrating them. Bishop Galen's disclosures struck a responsive chord and copies of the sermon were distributed throughout the Reich. His popularity made it impossible for the government to proceed against him, although some officials did propose that his "treasonable actions" warranted the death penalty.

The regime had underestimated the possibility of such a public reaction and the far-reaching nature of its impact. Shortly after Galen's sermon, the "euthanasia" programme was officially halted by a *Führerbefehl* (command from the Führer) of 24 August 1941 – although "wild euthanasia" killings through starvation or lethal "medication" continued. These public protests helped to form and consolidate public opinion, contributed to the general feeling of outrage, and led to the suspension of the "euthanasia" campaign. Thus the public conscience could still assert itself even in 1941 when an issue affected the lives of Germans and their families. The subsequent disaster which befell the Jews, the culmination of a poisonous and unrelenting anti-Semitic propaganda, did not give rise to the same ostensible debate or public outcry.

Hitler's readiness to authorize the "euthanasia action", coupled with his virulent and life-long hatred of Jews which gave rise to his "prophecy" of January 1939 that the war would lead to the destruction of European Jewry, convinces me that his role in the "cumulative radicalization" of anti-Jewish policy was both central and fundamental. Yet no written directive from Hitler authorizing the "Final Solution" has been discovered, even after the opening of the former Soviet archives. Does the absence of such a written directive invalidate the claim that Hitler personally ordered the extermination of European Jewry? Arguably, because of the difficulties Hitler had encountered with the "euthanasia" action, he would have been reluctant to have given written authorization for the more radical solution to the so-called "Jewish Question". Hitler was an intuitive politician and would have recognized the high stakes involved. While he remained the inspiration behind the "Final Solution" he wanted it to be kept secret. Thus a circumlocutory language was invented to camouflage what was actually taking place and this served to distance Hitler from these actions. The lack of a written directive ordering the "Final Solution" is frankly a red herring that fails to recognize Hitler's character, his style of leadership and the way "charismatic authority" functioned in the Third Reich. His verbal approval (and/or any subsequent sign of disapproval) was sufficient to unleash initiatives "from below". Moreover there was no need (for him) to provide written authorization as he knew that numerous "little Hitlers", "working towards the Führer", would implement his totalitarian vision without written authority.

If Hitler was to maintain his deified status as the benign Führer then he could not become too involved in day-to-day politics. Instead, officials would have to "work towards the Führer". Werner Willikens, a Nazi official in the Ministry of Agriculture, set out precisely what this meant in a speech in 1934:

> Everyone who has the opportunity to observe it knows that the Führer can hardly dictate from above everything which he intends to realize ... On the contrary, up till now everyone with a post in the new Germany has worked best when he has, so to speak, worked towards the Führer. Very often and in many spheres it has been the case ... that individuals have simply waited for orders and instructions. Unfortunately, the same will be true in the future; but in fact it is the duty of everybody to try to work towards the Führer along the lines he would wish. Anyone who makes mistakes will notice it soon enough. But anyone who really works towards the Führer along his lines and towards his goal will certainly both now and in the future one day have the finest reward in the form of the sudden legal confirmation of his work. (Noakes & Pridham vol. 2 (1984): 207)

The process of "working towards the Führer" was driven by the tacit understanding that Hitler's wishes served to activate and legitimize initiatives from below. Such actions could encompass everything from a Hitler Youth denouncing his parents in the name of his Führer father-figure, doctors carrying out sterilization and "mercy-killings" in the name of the utopian racial community, "ordinary" citizens denouncing neighbours to the Gestapo for "un-Germanlike" behaviour, and judges progressively eroding the rule of law for personal advancement to the "Grand Inquisitor of European Jewry", Adolf Eichmann, who claimed at his trial that "personally" he had nothing against Jews but was merely a "conscientious civil servant" carrying out the wishes of his master. Eichmann was also "working towards the Führer". The notion of "working towards the Führer" ensured that policy could be carried out in accordance with Hitler's wishes without requiring his direct involvement or written authorization. As Willikens pointed out in 1934, the Führer would soon make it known if actions carried out in his name did not meet with his approval.

Richard Breitman, in his work on Himmler and the "Final Solution", has demonstrated that very little happened without Hitler's knowledge. Certain key decisions on the road to Auschwitz could only have been taken by Hitler. The logistics involved in slaughter on this scale required a considerable degree of collaboration within a mutually antagonistic political system. Only Hitler was in a position to force competing authorities to resolve their differences. Hitler's ideological drive made it possible to persuade other agencies, including the Wehrmacht, to co-operate with the SS in implementing the "Final Solution". Given the highly competitive nature of the "Führer state" this extraordinary degree of collaboration could only have been achieved if all the agencies involved believed that they were implementing the wishes of the Führer. The SS, the most dynamic and ideologically driven sector of the regime, stood outside control of any government ministry. Dependent solely upon Hitler, it justified itself as an executive agency of the "will of the Führer". Faced with opposition or hindrance of any kind the SS was able to legitimize its actions by recourse to the Führer's "mission" and its plenipotentiary powers bestowed by Hitler. Breitman concludes that Himmler, the head of the SS, may have been the "architect" of genocide but he was no more than an instrument of Hitler's will.

We know from anecdotal evidence, especially the diaries of Joseph Goebbels and the evidence of Eichmann at his trial in 1960, that Hitler was fully aware and approved of the extermination of the Jews. For example, in March 1942 Goebbels wrote of "a life-and-death struggle between the Aryan race and the Jewish bacillus" and referred to Hitler as "the undismayed champion of a radical solution". A month later Goebbels was reporting Hitler as being "unrelenting" in his desire to rid Europe of Jews. We know also from Himmler's appointment book that was recently discovered in the former Soviet archives that Himmler met with Hitler on 18 December 1941 to discuss the "Jewish Question" (*Judenfrage*) and that in the course of the conversation their "extermination" was mentioned. Many decisions such as the introduction of the yellow star to be worn by German Jews and extending the killing in the Soviet Union to include women and children (both in August 1941) were explicity approved by Hitler. Hitler also took the decision to deport German Jews to the east in September 1941. The fate of these Jews was sealed and the deportation of western European Jewry began in earnest in the winter of 1941–2.

Philippe Burrin, who has subjected Hitler's personal role in the genesis of the Holocaust to a detailed and penetrating analysis, has convincingly argued that in late August and early September 1941, as the war in the Soviet Union began to falter, Hitler returned to his Reichstag "prophecy" of January 1939 that the war would end in the "destruction of European Jewry". Having failed to capture Moscow, an increasingly frustrated Hitler recognized that an all-out victory was far from inevitable, and that the escalation into mass extermination symbolized a total commitment to fight to the end. Hitler's state of mind is therefore of considerable importance in the chronology of how this decision was reached. By mid September 1941, according to Burrin, Hitler's mood, shaped by an increasing awareness of failure, was degenerating into deep pessimism (Burrin 1994). Christopher Browning, while agreeing with Burrin that late September was the crucial period, argues that Hitler's decision was driven not by a sense of failure but by one of renewed military optimism generated by victories in the Ukraine (Browning 1992). I am personally persuaded by the weight of evidence suggesting that Hitler gave the verbal approval, or possibly even a written instruction, in either late September or early October 1941. In all probability it was disseminated via Heydrich's office in the Reich Security Headquarters. However, Christian Gerlach has recently unleashed a new debate by claiming that Hitler did give an order for the total extermination of European Jewry at a conference for Nazi Party leaders on 12 December 1941, following Germany's declaration of war on the United States of America (Gerlach 1997, 1998). Based on a notation by Heinrich Himmler, discovered in previously secret Soviet archives, Gerlach argues that Hitler's decision was prompted in part by America's entry into the war after the Japanese attack on Pearl Harbor on 7 December 1941. In his declaration of war speech to the Reichstag on 11 December, which was broadcast on the radio, Hitler did not mention extermination but referred only to Jewish warmongers "hovering behind Roosevelt". Besieged by requests from Party leaders to define which categories of Jews should be put to death in the east, Hitler decided it was time to redeem his "prophecy" of January 1939 that a world war would mean the destruction of all Europe's Jews, not just those in the Soviet Union (Gerlach 1997, 1998). Goebbels attended the meeting convened by Hitler on the afternoon of 12 December and recorded in his diary:

> Regarding the Jewish Question the Führer is resolved to make a clean sweep. He has prophesied to the Jews that, if they were to bring about once more a World War, it would result in their annihilation. That was no hollow phrase. The World War is here, the annihilation of Jewry must be the necessary consequence. (Goebbels Diaries, ed. Fröhlich, vol. 2: 498, entry 13 December 1941)

For Gerlach the announcement of a decision on 12 December 1941 was an inexorable step on the path to genocide. It is, he writes, a crucial missing piece of the decision-making process leading up to the liquidation of the Jews of Europe: 'Hitler's decision put the planning for these crimes on a new basis' (Gerlach 1998: 809).

Outside a small group of perpetrators selected to carry out Hitler's orders, it was imperative to maintain a blanket of silence. The mounting military defeats that ensued lent an added urgency to resolve the "Jewish Question". For many Nazi officials there was now an even bigger fear in the light of what had already taken place: that if the war was lost, surviving Jews would return to Germany and extract a terrible revenge. Himmler even justified the murder of Jewish women and children along the lines that the Nazis "could not allow a generation of avengers to grow up". The accelerating rate of slaughter can be explained by the momentum generated by the deteriorating exigencies of war and the opportunites thus offered to activists on the ground to exceed and surpass their "killing-quotas". Fanatical "desk-murderers" in the SS, like Adolf Eichmann, could seize on the chaos unleashed by a no-holds-barred war of extermination and continuously set ever higher targets.

Acknowledging Hitler's pivotal role in the "cumulative radicalization" of anti-Jewish policy from incremental persecution to genocide does not mean that we have to assume that a clear plan and timetable for the extermination of the Jews always existed. If it existed at all it existed in Hitler's mind. "Intentionalist" historians like Lucy Dawidowicz and Gerald Fleming claim that a "programmatist" line can be drawn that links Hitler's early anti-Semitism to the Holocaust. For Dawidowicz, Hitler's "grand design" can be traced to his experiences in the Pasewalk hospital in 1918 when he was recovering from mustard gas. Fleming takes the line back even further to the shaping of Hitler's anti-Semitism in Linz in the period 1904–7. Both believe that Hitler possessed a blueprint for annihilation when he came to power and that he never wavered in realizing these ideological goals. Other historians like Karl Schleunes prefer to talk about a "twisted" road to Auschwitz marked by opportunism, hesitancy and stops and starts. Most historians would agree that the war, and particularly the war against the Soviet Union, acted as a catalyst and allowed Hitler to justify the radicalization of his anti-Jewish policy and "realize the unthinkable". Implicit in Hitler's "prophecy" speech of January 1939 was a belief that war legitimized mass murder. Goebbels confirmed this when he wrote in his diary on 27 March 1942 that "a whole series of possibilities presents itself to us in wartime which would be denied us in peacetime" (Lochner 1948: 103). What might have happened without the war is hypothetical and irrelevant. However in stressing the centrality of Hitler to the Holocaust, in arguing emphatically that it would not have been implemented without his obsessive anti-Semitic "visions", one does not absolve others of complicity as well. The implementation of the "Final Solution" cannot be attributed to Hitler alone. It did happen and there can be no apologists for the Holocaust.

If one accepts that Hitler's race dogma was fundamental to Nazi genocide, this begs the question: how could Hitler's *Weltanschauung* have penetrated so many sections of German society and turned them into "willing executioners"? These are questions that lie outside the scope of this book. I will say, however, that Daniel Goldhagen's recent mono-causal explanation that a peculiarly virulent and deep-rooted anti-Semitism marked German culture from the medieval period onwards is both flawed and simplistic. According to Gold-hagen this variant strand of anti-Semitism had become so entrenched in German social mentality by the beginning of the nineteenth century that a genocidal or 'eliminationist' form of anti-Semitism took root which led *inevitably* towards repression, removal and ultimately 'extermination' . In other words it was not the case that Hitler's state succeeded in gradually persuading sufficient numbers to participate in the Holocaust – far from it, the Nazis merely opened the floodgates –

enabling the Gemans to implement their 'eliminationist' anti-Semitism. Goldhagen's book provided a new demonizing variation on the German *Sonderweg* ('special path' that is divergent from other western cultures) thesis that talked about a uniquely German brand of anti-Semitism (Goldhagen 1996).

In attempting to explain the Holocaust it cannot be argued rationally that anti-Semitism was a result of National Socialism or that Hitler made Germans anti-Semitic, but the fact remains that the Third Reich was responsible for genocide of unparalleled scope and brutality. There is very little in the German past that could seriously lead one to conclude that under certain circumstances a Holocaust was "waiting to happen". Germany was no more anti-Semitic than many other European nations (compare the anti-Semitism implicit in the Dreyfus affair in France in the late 1890s or the anti-Semitic pogroms in Tsarist Russia under Nicholas II). Comparative studies of anti-Semitism across Europe before 1933 have been extensive enough to cast serious doubt on the alleged uniqueness of the German variant. Nor can it be claimed that social Darwinist and eugenicist ideas were confined to Germany. Tragically, however, following the Nazi assumption of power, voices of protest, notably from the Left, which had traditionally championed minorities, were silenced and the full weight of the state fell in behind a concerted and relentless propaganda campaign that depicted Jews (and Slavs) as sub-human "parasites" that needed to be exterminated. To this end, the propaganda was greatly facilitated by the fact that it was being disseminated in a closed political environment, cut off from the outside world. Thus when the Nazis came to power they chose the Jews as a permanent scapegoat on which those in the Movement could work off their resentment. Therefore an important negative function of anti-Semitic propaganda was to divert public attention from the economic and social measures that the regime had promised but failed to deliver.

The scale of the crimes committed in Hitler's name is beyond normal comprehension and transcends human decency. No amount of archival film footage or survivor testimony can adequately convey the depths of human suffering and tragedy that must have been experienced in the death camps. Moreover, it is a human tragedy confined not only to the victims. The perpetrators of these crimes appeared to lose all sense of humanity. SS units, fuelled by Hitler's paranoid hatred and fear of Jews, developed within their ranks a quite extraordinary and incomprehensible *esprit de corps* that apparently buttressed them from the full horror of their actions. The executioners had depersonalized their victims to such an extent that Jews were viewed as animals in human form. Heinrich Himmler, for example, the supreme overseer of the "Final Solution", rationalized mass extermination in a manner that included no sense of guilt or shame. The language of genocide is nowhere more graphically illustrated than in his notorious speech of 4 October 1943 to SS Group Leaders in Poznan:

> One principle must be absolute for the SS man: we must be honest, decent, loyal, and comradely to members of our own blood and to no one else ... Whether the other peoples live in comfort or perish of hunger interests me only in so far as we need them as slaves for our *Kultur*. Whether or not 10,000 Russian women collapse from exhaustion while digging a tank ditch interests me only in so far as the tank ditch is completed for Germany ... We Germans, who are the only people in the world who have a decent attitude to animals, will also adopt a decent attitude to these human animals ... I shall speak to you here with frankness of a very grave matter. Among ourselves it should be mentioned quite frankly, and yet we will never speak of it publicly. I mean the evacuation of the Jews, the extermination of the Jewish people ... Most of you know what it means to see a hundred corpses lying together, five hundred, or a thousand. To have stuck it out and at the same time – apart from exceptions caused by human weakness – to have remained decent fellows, that is what is hard. This is a page of glory in our history which has never been written and shall never be written. (quoted Wistrich 1995: 113–4)

Historians who question Hitler's involvement in the day-to-day implementation of genocide point to the fact that precisely when the "Final Solution" was being implemented, Hitler became an increasingly remote figure. Helmut Heiber has even referred to him as the "part-time Chancellor" (Heiber 1962: 32). Although Hitler is widely associated with orchestrating the war and the Holocaust, it is true that from the end of 1941 onwards he became physically detached for much of the time from the hub of government in Berlin. His health also deteriorated under the impact of the drugs prescribed by his quack physician Dr Morell. Refusing to countenance military defeat, Hitler became even more prone to irrational outbursts (largely aimed at his generals). Defeat at Stalingrad where General von Paulus's Sixth Army was cut off and surrendered to the Russians in January 1943 represented a devastating blow to Hitler. His prestige in the eyes of the German people suffered even more when he refused to address the nation who held him personally responsible for the defeat. Writing in his diary in March 1943, Goebbels referred to Hitler as "tragic" and "reclusive" and even spoke to Albert Speer of a "leader crisis". By 1942 Hitler was unquestionably a sick man. Portents of his own mortality may well have strengthened his resolve to fulfil his ideological objectives. Hitler's all-consuming anti-Semitism is enshrined in his last "Political Testament", a document he dictated in the bunker of the Reich Chancellery shortly before he took his life on 30 April 1945. He remained what he had always been, a virulent anti-Semite who attributed all historical and political misfortunes to the Jews: "Above all, I enjoin the government and the people to uphold the race laws to the limit and to resist mercilessly the poisoner of all nations, international Jewry." These were his final words in his last testament. He died cursing the Jews.

Conclusion

If I may paraphrase Oscar Wilde's Algernon in *The Importance of Being Earnest*, "The truth about Hitler is rarely pure and never simple." He was in every sense of the word a most unlovely man. He was nihilistic and brutal. He also possessed the traits of the fastidious and bigoted petit-bourgeois. There is something almost comic about this side of his personality – a sort of Austro-German "disgusted from Linz". Much of his writing is in the didactic style and his *Table talk* reads like the ramblings of a retired and incoherent major looking back to some mythological past. In the case of Adolf Hitler, however, his long-standing prejudices and opinions were not confined to the letter pages of national newspapers. Nevertheless, the ridiculous side of Hitler's character should not be overlooked or underestimated because of the horrors that he instigated. It is precisely the juxtaposition of undistiguished ordinariness and indescribable wickedness that is so striking. Hannah Arendt was making a similar point when she talked about the "banality of evil" (Arendt 1958).

Writing some years ago, Michael Kater commented that our understanding of Nazism "has hardly been advanced by the spate of biographies of Hitler". While I have attempted to avoid the pitfall of another biography I have not ignored personal factors in Hitler's life. Instead I have attempted to concentrate on the interaction of personal and impersonal factors in determining Nazi policy. It is important, I believe, to look at the impact on government of the "charismatic" rule of Hitler, his "visions" and his actions. The personality cult of Hitler cannot be dismissed for it is essential to the "ideology" of the NSDAP. The doctrine adopted by the Nazi Party became inseparable from Hitler's *Weltanschauung* that had been firmly established by the mid 1920s and rarely changed. Nevertheless, Hitler's messianic belief in his own "mission" shaped a pragmatism that was prepared to cynically disregard programmes and principles except as a means to power. Once he gained power Hitler never had any intention of becoming a prisoner of the governmental system. His power resided in the office of Führer. Invoking Hitler's name was like opening a door – a gateway to power. In this way, by delegating power downwards but in a random fashion based on access to the Führer, Hitler was able to outflank the traditional bureaucracy of government and civil service. By creating his own bureaucratic hierarchies operating side by side with the more traditional elites, Hitler actively encouraged "little Hitlers" to mark out their own territories and abuse their power – provided they did not threaten his own position as Führer.

Simply because historians have moved away from the monolithic totalitarian model and have stressed instead the "permanent improvisation and chaos" of Hitler's rule does not prove that Hitler was a "weak dictator". Hitler chose not to be involved in the day-to-day affairs of state. Such a policy suited his style of leadership, allowing him to make arbitrary interventions and forcing his subordinates to continually second-guess his intentions. I can think of no examples of major policy decisions by Hitler being successfully thwarted by ministers or civil servants.

By the late 1920s, Hitler had become indispensable to the Movement. The towering ego of the man had swept aside all rivals. Much of his charismatic authority within the Party rested on the bonds of loyalty that had been established through participation in the ill-fated Munich *Putsch* of 1923. When he became Chancellor in 1933 this same loyalty was expressed in mystical terms like "working towards the Führer". Not only did Hitler's charismatic authority serve as a benchmark for rank-and-file activists but it also served to check the ambitions and jealousies within the Nazi fiefdoms. The deeds of the old fighting comrades who took part in the *Putsch* and later in the "time of struggle" were mythologized in the Third Reich. The continuing loyalty of this group of "fighting comrades" remained important to Hitler. With the exception of the "Night of the Long Knives" in 1934, Hitler did not go in for purges in the same way that Stalin did. Generals, politicains, diplomats who had displeased Hitler would normally be "retired" gracefully from the scene.

This bond of loyalty only began to disintegrate in the final months of the Third Reich. It is extraordinary to record that many of his generals continued to the end to take orders from a mentally deranged dictator dispensing wild and irresponsible instructions from deep within his bunker in the Reich Chancellery. The same hatred and fear which had led to mass extermination was now turned on his own people. In the last weeks of the war, Hitler's vindictive and senseless "Nero Order" for a "scorched earth" policy in the face of the advancing Allied armies was only prevented by Albert Speer's successful sabotage. A small group from within the Nazi elite, including Himmler and Göring, did attempt in the last days of the war to sue for peace without Hitler's knowledge. This represented for Hitler the ultimate treachery and in his last "Political Testament" he expelled them both from the Party, stating: "Apart altogether from their disloyalty to me, Göring and Himmler have brought irreparable shame on the whole nation by secretly negotiating with the enemy without my knowledge and against my will, and also by attempting illegally to seize control of the State" (Maser 1976: 354). Hitler's capacity for self-delusion had been evident since the mid 1920s. To the very end he would not accept responsibility for Germany's defeat. He declared shortly before taking his own life and that of his bride, Eva Braun, that "If the German people loses the war, it will have proved itself not worthy of me".

While focusing on the negative aspects of Hitler's rule it is equally important to remember his enduring popularity. Hitler exacted an extraordinary degree of loyalty and affection. How can this be explained? In 1941, at the height of Germany's military success, Goebbels informed his officials in the Propaganda Ministry that his two notable propaganda achievements were, first, "the style and technique of the Party's public ceremonies; the ceremonial of the mass demonstrations, the ritual of the great Party occasion", and, second, that through his "creation of the Führer-myth, Hitler had been given the halo of infallibility, with the result that many people who looked askance at the Party after 1933 had now complete confidence in Hitler" (Welch 1995: 86–7). Hitler was indeed the most vital legitimizing force within the regime.

By appearing to stand above the day-to-day realities of the regime, Hitler acted as a kind of medieval monarch, as a positive symbol, a focus of loyalty and of national unity. Hitler was presented as not just another party leader but as the leader for whom Germany had been waiting – a leader who would place the nation before any particularist cause. The nature of Hitler's position as charismatic leader, as the Führer of the German people, rested on his continuing ability to detach himself from day-to-day politics with the result that he was never personally associated with the worst extremes of the regime. Different social groupings, ranging from the industrial working class to church leaders, continued to perceive Hitler as a "moderate", opposed to the radical and extreme elements within the Movement. One of the most significant achievements of the propaganda construction of the Führer-myth was the success in separating Hitler from the growing unpopularity of the Nazi Party itself. The secret reports of the Social Democratic Party in exile (Sopade), for example, show that the Fuhrer-myth was a genuinely integratory force in society after 1933, penetrating even into sections of the working class who opposed the Nazi Party itself, and eliciting an extraordinary degree of loyalty to Hitler. According to the Secret Police reports, this loyalty only began to disintegrate after Stalingrad and the refusal of Hitler to address the nation. Even as late as 1944 Goebbels achieved a short-lived revival of trust in the Führer following the failure of the 20 July plot against him. The abortive attempt on Hitler's life was widely greeted with shock and horror and enabled Goebbels to exploit the attempted assassination to show that the hand of Providence was guiding Hitler by coining the slogan "Hitler is Victory" ("*Hitler ist der Sieg*"). As late as 29 April 1945, Berlin newspapers were still insisting that Hitler would remain steadfast with his people and "wherever the Führer is, there is victory".

Nonetheless, Goebbels' manipulatory skill alone could not have created the quasi-religious faith in Hitler demonstrated by large sections of the German population. Without concrete achievements Hitler could not have sustained his positive image as Führer. By the spring of 1939 Sopade were identifying the reduction in unemployment and a series of foreign policy successes as the two major achievements consolidating Hitler's position. In domestic politics, Hitler was recognized for having won the "Battle for Work", building the Autobahns, and generally revamping the economy. Although industrial workers continued to view the "economic miracle" in terms of longer hours and low wages, nevertheless they welcomed the restoration of full employment and the social welfare schemes for the poorer sections of the community. The middle class, who had benefited from the rearmament boom of the mid 1930s, remained devoted to Hitler whom they saw as the father-figure of the regime.

Much of Hitler's popularity since he came to power rested on his achievements in foreign policy. A recurring theme in Nazi propaganda before 1939 was that Hitler was a man of peace but one who was determined to recover German territories "lost" as a result of the Versailles Treaty. Providing foreign policy propaganda could show the achievements of revisionism without German bloodshed, then it was relatively easy to feast upon the consensus that favoured overthrowing the humiliation of the post-war peace settlements. From the moment in 1936 when Hitler ordered German troops to re-occupy the demilitarized Rhineland until the Munich agreement in 1938 which gave the Sudentenland to Germany, Hitler had successfully carried out a series of audacious foreign policy coups that won him support from all sections of the community. He was now widely acclaimed, enjoying unparalleled popularity and prestige. However, there was a basic contradiction between propaganda that presented the Führer as a "man of peace" and an ideology that was inexorably linked to struggle and war.

When the war came, Hitler's astonishing run of *Blitzkrieg* victories, culminating in the fall of France, confirmed Hitler's standing as a military strategist of genius who even confounded his own generals. When the war started to turn against him in the winter of 1941–2 it would take some time before military reverses had any noticeable effect on his popularity. Although the standing of his Party dropped considerably, Hitler's personal standing remained remarkably high. However, following the catastrophe of Stalingrad, a defeat for which Hitler was held responsible, his popularity began to decline. With no new military victories to talk of, Hitler retreated into his bunker. In the final year of the war Goebbels attempted to resurrect the Führer-cult by depicting Hitler as a latter-day Frederick the Great, ultimately triumphant in the face of adversity. This absurd image in the face of the gathering Russian occupation of Germany represented an alarming flight from reality that no amount of propaganda could sustain. The Hitler myth and "charismatic leadership" could not survive such lack of success, and were on the verge of extinction.

Finally, there is the question of the relevance (or otherwise) of Hitler to contemporary society. Should we view Hitler as a warning from history? To understand Hitler's appeal and his role in the government of the Third Reich we have to place his ideas and actions in the context of a defeated and humiliated post-1918 Germany. Hitler was the product of a historically unique set of circumstances. By studying Hitler we learn a great deal about conditions that existed particularly in Germany – but also in Europe generally – in the middle part of the twentieth century. To personalize history and to hold Hitler solely responsible for crimes committed by a regime over which he presided is not only an oversimplification; it also absolves others of guilt. Kershaw has memorably written that "the road to Auschwitz was built by hate, but paved with indifference" (Kershaw 1983: 277). Hitler's racist vision was pivotal in the road to Auschwitz but to fully understand how the Holocaust came about one would need to analyze the conditions that allowed for apathy and indifference to take root in Germany. Adolf Hitler was a dictator different from those in history that preceeded him and those that followed him. Despite our knowledge of Hitler, it did not prevent an Idi Amin or a Pol Pot emerging in the post-1945 world. Furthermore, genocide did not end with the collapse of the Third Reich. For historians, Hitler remains endlessly fascinating and his motivations obscurantist. But equally he is almost an irrelevance to the contemporary political commentator. There are real dangers in comparing contemporary figures with historical despots. In the 1950s when President Nasser of Egypt attempted to nationalize the Suez Canal, British officials blindly compared Nasser to Hitler and concluded that dictators should not be appeased. The result was a wholly unnecessary and misguided war in the Middle East that ended in humiliation for Britain. One of the great strengths of studying history is that it frees us from the tyranny of present mindedness. That is not to say that the past has no relevance for the present. As the German philosopher, Karl Jaspers, has poignantly reminded us, "That which has happened is a warning. To forget is guilt."

Adolf Hitler (1889–1945) Timeline

1889	Hitler's birth
1903	Death of father Alois Schickelgruber Hitler
1906	Hitler's first visit to Vienna
1907	Hitler takes up residence in Vienna
1908	Death of Hitler's mother, Klara
1913	Hitler moves to Munich
1914	Outbreak of First World War
16 August	Joins Reserve Infantry Regiment
2 December	Awarded Iron Cross 2nd Class
1918	
4 August	Awarded Iron Cross 1st Class
23 October	Temporarily blinded by mustard gas
9 November	Abdication of Kaiser Wilhelm II
1919	Setting up of the Weimar Republic
28 June	Signing of the Treaty of Versailles
16 September	Hitler joins the German Workers' Party (later renamed National Socialist German Workers' Party – NSDAP)

1921

5 October   Formation of SA (*Sturmabteilung* – stormtroopers
                   – formerly known as *Sports Abteilung*)

1923

8–9 November   *Putsch* in Munich and Hitler's arrest

1924   Hitler in prison; *Mein Kampf* written

1925

26 February   The Nazi Party re-founded
18 July   Volume I of *Mein Kampf* published

1926

10 December   Volume II of *Mein Kampf* published

1928

28 May   NSDAP attain 2.6 per cent of vote in Reichstag
                   elections (12 seats)
June–July   Dictated *Second Book*

1929   Wall Street Crash and onset of Depression

1930

30 March   Brüning becomes Chancellor of minority govern-
                   ment following resignation of Social Democrats
                   (SPD)
14 September   Nazi breakthrough in Reichstag elections; NSDAP
                   gain 18.8 per cent of vote and 107 seats

1932

13 March   Hindenburg fails to to attain absolute majority in
                   presidential elections (49.6 per cent compared to
                   Hitler's 30.1 per cent)
10 April   Hindenburg defeats Hitler again in second elec-
                   tion with 53 per cent; Hitler's vote increases to
                   36.8 per cent
13 April   SA and SS banned
May–June   Brüning resigns as Chancellor and is replaced by
                   Franz von Papen

31 July	Further Nazi successes in Reichstag elections, gaining 37.3 per cent of the vote and 230 seats, becoming largest single party in the Reichstag
6 November	Fall in Nazi support in Reichstag elections to 33.1 per cent and 197 seats but remain strongest party
December	Schleicher appointed Chancellor

1933

30 January	Hitler appointed Chancellor
27 February	Reichstag fire leading to suspension of civil rights
5 March	Reichstag elections: Nazis win 43.9 per cent of the vote and 288 seats
23 March	Enabling Law passed
April	Boycott of Jewish shops began; the German states or *Länder* are "co-ordinated"
2 May	Trade Unions banned
14 July	Political parties banned
20 July	Concordat with the Papacy
12 November	Reichstag "elections" and referendum; Nazis won 92.3 per cent of the vote and in plebiscite, 95.1 per cent support decision to leave League of Nations

1934

26 January	Non-aggression treaty between Germany and Poland
30 June	"Night of the Long Knives": Röhm and several political opponents murdered
2 August	Death of Hindenburg. Hitler nominated Führer; approved by 89.9 per cent in accompanying plebiscite (19 August)

1935

13 January	Saar Plebiscite – over 90 per cent in favour of returning to Germany
16 March	Reintroduction of conscription
15 September	Nuremberg Laws against the Jews; Reich Citizenship Laws

1936

7 March	Reoccupation of demilitarized Rhineland
29 March	Reichstag "election": 99 per cent support for Hitler
1 August	Olympic Games in Berlin
9 September	Announcement of Four-Year Plan
November	Rome–Berlin Axis and Anti-Comintern Pact between Germany and Japan

1937

5 November	The Hossbach Conference

1938

4 February	Dismissal of the War Minister, von Blomberg, and the Commander-in-Chief, von Fritsch; Hitler appoints himself supreme commander of Wehrmacht
10 April	Over 99 per cent in plebiscite support *Anschluss* with Austria
29–30 September	Meetings with Chamberlain at Berchtesgaden and Godesberg; Munich Agreement over Czechoslovakia
October	German troops occupy the Sudetenland
9–10 November	"Kristallnacht": attacks on Jewish property

1939

30 January	Hitler makes his "prophecy" on the fate of Jews to Reichstag
14–15 March	German occupation of Czechoslovakia
23 March	German occupation of Memel
22 May	Pact of Steel between Germany and Italy
23 August	Non-aggression Pact between Germany and USSR
1 September	German invasion of Poland
3 September	Britain and France declare war on Germany
8 November	Assassination attempt on Hitler in Munich

1940

9 April	German invasion of Denmark and Norway
10 May	German invasion of Netherlands, Belgium, Luxembourg and France

22 June	French signed Armistice at Compiègne
16 July	Preparation set out for invasion of Britain (Operation Sealion); postponed indefinitely following day
31 July	Hitler informs military leaders of his plans to invade USSR (Operation Barbarossa)

1941

6 April	German invasion of Yugoslavia and Greece
6 June	"Commissar Order" to liquidate Soviet Political Commissars
22 June	German invasion of USSR
1 September	German Jews compelled to wear yellow star of David (following on from Polish Jews who had been wearing the star since 23 November 1939)
14 October	Order to deport German Jews to eastern ghettos
December	Mass killing of Jews using mobile gas vans in Chelmno, Poland
11 December	German declaration of war on USA
16 December	Hitler appointed himself Commander-in-Chief of the army

1942

20 January	Wannsee Conference co-ordinates the "Final Solution"
March	Implementation of "Operation Reinhard" at Belzec and the first mass killings of Jews from the ghettos in Poland
June	Start of mass gassing of Jews in Auschwitz-Birkenau
5 October	Himmler orders deportation of all Jews from concentration camps in the Reich to Auschwitz
November	German defeat at El Alamein; Allied landings in North Africa

1943

31 Jan–2 Feb	German surrender at Stalingrad
18 February	Goebbels' declaration of "Total War"
13 May	German surrender in North Africa

July	Allied landings in Sicily and overthrow of Mussolini

1944

6 June	Allied landings in Normandy
22 June	Massive Wehrmacht losses in face of major Soviet offensive
20 July	Unsuccessful bomb plot against Hitler
1 November	Himmler orders ending of gassings in Auschwitz-Birkenau and removal of all traces of extermination

1945

12 January	Major Soviet offensive against German eastern front
30 January	Hitler's last broadcast
19 March	Hitler's "Nero Order" of "scorched earth" to destroy what remained of Germany's infrastructure
29–30 April	Hitler's marriage to Eva Braun, his last "Political Testament" and suicide in the bunker of the Reich Chancellery in Berlin
May	Unconditional surrender of Germany

Select bibliography

General historiographical surveys

Ayçoberry, P. *The Nazi question* (London, 1981.)

Frei, N. *National socialist rule in Germany: the Führer State 1933–45* (London, 1993).

Hiden, J. and Farquharson, J. *Explaining Hitler's Germany: historians and the Third Reich* (London, 1984; 2nd edn 1989).

Housden, M. *Resistance and conformity in the Third Reich* (London, 1996): a wide-ranging collection of sources with detailed analysis.

Kater, M. "Hitler in a social context", *Central European History* vol. 14 (1981), 243–72.

Kershaw, I. *The Nazi dictatorship: problems and perspectives of interpretation* (London, 1985, 3rd edn 1993): the most comprehensive and penetrating analysis available.

Noakes, J. and Pridham, G. (eds) *Nazism 1919–1945. A documentary reader* (4 vols, Exeter, 1983–8): a simply indispensable source book with an excellent commentary.

Wistrich, R. *Who's who in Nazi Germany* (London, 1995): a reliable and perceptive reference guide.

The rise of the NSDAP

Allen, W.S. *The Nazi seizure of power: the experience of a single German town*, 1930–35 (Chicago, 1965).

Bessel, R. *Political violence and the rise of Nazism* (New Haven/London, 1984).

Bohnke, W. *Die NSDAP im Ruhrgebiet 1920–33* (Bonn-Bad Godesberg, 1974).

Broszat, M. *Hitler and the collapse of Weimar Germany* (Leamington Spa, 1987).

Childers, T. "The social bases of the national socialist vote", *Journal of Contemporary History* vol. 11 (1976), 17–42.

Childers, T. *The Nazi voter* (Chapel Hill, 1983): probably the best book to date on factors contributing to Nazi electoral success.

Childers, T. (ed.) *The formation of the Nazi constituency 1919–1933* (London/Sydney, 1986).

Fischer, C. "The SA of the NSDAP: social background and ideology of the rank and file in the early 1930s", *Journal of Contemporary History* vol. 17 (1982), 651–70.

Fischer, C. *The rise of the Nazis* (Manchester 1995): an excellent guide to an extremely complex topic. Includes a number of primary documents.

Hamilton, R.F. *Who voted for Hitler?* (Princeton, 1982).

Kater, M. *The Nazi Party: a social profile of members and leaders 1919–1945* (Oxford, 1983).

Kehr, H. & Langmaid, J. *The Nazi era 1919–1945* (London, 1982).

Mühlberger, D. *Hitler's followers: studies in the sociology of the Nazi movement* (London, 1991).

Noakes, J. *The Nazi Party in Lower Saxony 1921–33* (Oxford, 1971).

Orlow, D. *The history of the Nazi Party 1919–33* (London, 1971).

Pridham, G. *Hitler's rise to power: the Nazi movement in Bavaria 1923–33* (London, 1973).

Stachura, P.D. *Gregor Strasser and the rise of Nazism* (London, 1983): sets in perspective the important part played by Gregor Strasser before 1932.

Stachura, P. (ed.) *The Nazi Machtergreifung 1933* (London, 1983).

Turner, H.A. Jr. *Hitler's thirty days to power: January 1933* (London, 1996): a fascinating account of the intrigues that allowed Hitler into power.

Hitler

Baynes, N.H. (ed.) *The speeches of Adolf Hitler* (2 vols, Oxford, 1942).

Binion, R. *Hitler among the Germans* (New York, 1976).

Bracher, K.D. *The German dictatorship: the origins, structure and consequences of national socialism* (London, 1973).

Bracher, K.D. "The role of Hitler: perspectives of interpretation", in W. Laqueur (ed.) *Fascism: a reader's guide* (London, 1979), 193–212.

Broszat, M. *Der Staat Hitlers* (Munich, 1969), translated as *The Hitler state: the foundation and development of the internal structure of the Third Reich* (London, 1981).

Bullock, A. *Hitler: a study in tyranny* (London, 1952; rev. edn, 1964): although somewhat dated now since it was written in 1952, this remains a powerful biography.

Bullock, A. *Parallel lives: Hitler and Stalin* (London, 1991): incorporates recent historical analysis and focuses more on the stucture of government; a perceptive comparative analysis with Stalin.

Bullock, A. "Personality and power: The strange case of Hitler and Stalin", German Historical Institute 1994 Annual Lecture (London, 1995), 5–25.

Carr, W. *Hitler: a study in personality and politics* (London, 1978): a much underrated analysis that provides a fascinating interpretation of the impact of Hitler's personality on decision-making.

Dietrich, O. *12 Jahre mit Hitler* (Munich, 1955), translated as *The Hitler I knew* (London, 1957).

Domarus, M. (ed.) *Hitler. Reden und Proklamationen 1932–45* (4 vols, Munich, 1965).

Domarus, M. (ed.) *Hitler's proclomations and speeches* (London, 1990): a long overdue translation of an important collection of documents.

Fest, J. *Hitler* (Frankfurt-am-Main, 1973), English translation (London, 1974): concentrates on the psychological forces driving Hitler's character; a useful complement to Bullock.

Fest J. *The face of the Third Reich* (London, 1974).

Fox, J. "Adolf Hitler: the continuing debate", *International Affairs 55* (1979).

Geary, D. *Hitler and Nazism* (London, 1993): despite its title, this pamphlet is more concerned with Nazism than with Hitler. Very strong on the economic factors that led to the collapse of the Weimar Republic and contributed to the Nazi electoral success.

Gordon, H.J. *Hitler and the Beer Hall Putsch* (Princeton, 1972).

Haffner, S. *The meaning of Hitler* (London, 1979): thought-provoking and controversial.

Hamann, B. *Hitlers Wien Lehrjahre eines Diktators* (Munich, 1996).

Hamann, B. *Hitler's Vienna: A Dictator's Apprenticeship* (OUP, 1999): magnificent work that corrects numerous misconceptions about Hitler's early years in Vienna.

Hanfstaengl, E. *Hitler: the missing years* (London, 1957).

Hauner, M. "Did Hitler want a world dominion?", *Journal of Contemporary History* vol. 13 No. 1 (January, 1978), 15–32.

Hesse, F. *Hitler and the English* (London, 1954).

Hirschfeld, G. & Kettenacker, L. (eds) *The "Fuhrer-State": myth and reality* (Stuttgart, 1981).

Hitler, A. *Mein Kampf* (Munich 1937, London, 1939).

Hitler, A. *Mein Kampf* with intro. by D.C. Watt (London, 1969).

Hitler, A. *Hitler's secret book* with intro. by T. Taylor (New York, 1961).

Hitler, A. *Hitler's letters and notes*, compiled and with commentary by Werner Maser (London, 1976).

Hitler, A. *Hitler's table talk 1941–44*, introduced and with a new Preface by H.R. Trevor-Roper (London, 1973).

Hoffmann, H. *Hitler was my friend* (London, 1955): written from the perspective of Hitler's photographer.

Housden, M. *Hitler. Study of a Revolutionary?* (London, 2000)

Jäckel, E. *Hitler's Weltanschauung: a blueprint for power* (Middleton/London, 1972).

Jäckel, E. *Hitler in history* (Hanover/London, 1984): a valuable and perceptive analysis of Hitler's personality.

James, J. & Barnes, P.P. *Hitler's "Mein Kampf" in Britain and America* (Cambridge, 1980).

Kershaw, I. *The "Hitler myth": image and reality in the Third Reich* (Oxford, 1987): an exploration of the basis of Hitler's popular support.

Kershaw, I. *Hitler* (London, 1991): a short, interpretative study that synthesizes much of Kershaw's pathfinding work.

Kershaw, I. "Ideologue and propagandist: Hitler in light of his speeches, writings and orders, 1925–1928", *Yad Vashem Studies* vol. XXIII (Jerusalem, 1993), 321–34.

Kershaw, I. " 'Working Towards the Führer': reflections on the nature of the Hitler dictatorship" *Contemporary European History*, 2, 2 (1993), 103–18.

Kershaw, I. *Hitler: vol. 1, Hubris, 1889–1937* (London, 1998).

Kershaw, I. *Hitler: vol. 2, Nemesis, 1938–45* (London, 2000).

Kettenacker, L. "Hitler's impact on the lower middle class", in D. Welch (ed.) *Nazi propaganda: the power and the limitations* (London, 1983).

Kubizek, A. *The Young Hitler I Knew* (Westport, Conn., 1955): his memoirs were originally commissioned by the NSDAP, nevertheless, provided it is read critically it provides a revealing insight into Hitler's early years.

Lukacs, J. *The Hitler of history* (New York, 1997).

Maser, W. *Hitler's letters and notes* (New York, 1976).

Peterson, E.N. *The limits of Hitler's power* (Princeton, 1969).

Rauschning, H. *Hitler speaks* (London, 1940): Rauschning was a supporter turned critic of Hitler. The authenticity of his records has been the source of acrimonious debate and some historians, notably Kershaw (1998), have decided to disregard the work.

Relich, F. *Hitler. Diagnosis of a Destructive Prophet* (Oxford, 1999).

Rosenbaum, R. *Explaining Hitler, the Search for the Origins of his Evil* (London, 1998).

Smith, B. *Adolf Hitler. His Family, Childhood, and Youth* (Stanford, 1967)

Stern, J.P. *Hitler: The Führer and the people* (London, 1975): largely forgotten and much underrated; explores Hitler as a "representative" individual within German society

Stokes, G. *Hitler and the quest for world domination: Nazi ideology and foreign policy in the 1920s* (Leamington Spa, 1987).

Stone, N. *Hitler* (London, 1980).

Taylor, A.J.P. *Europe: grandeur and decline* (London, 1979): a typically idiosyncratic essay on Hitler.

Thies, J. "Nazi architecture – a blueprint for world domination: the last aims of Adolf Hitler", in D. Welch (ed.) *Nazi propaganda: the power and the limitations* (London, 1983).

Toland, J. *Adolf Hitler* (New York, 1976).

Trevor-Roper, H.R. *The last days of Hitler* (London, 1962).

Waite, R. *The psychopathic god: Adolf Hitler* (New York, 1977): a speculative "psycho-historical" study.

Zitelmann, R. *Hitler. Selbstverständnis eines Revolutionärs* (Munich, 1989): a controversial biography that views Hitler as a revolutionary.

Foreign policy, the economy and war

Barkai, A. *Nazi economics: ideology, theory and policy* (Oxford, 1990).

Carr, W. *Arms, autarky, and aggression: a study in German foreign policy* (London, 1979).

Carroll, B.A. *Design for total war: arms and economics in the Third Reich* (The Hague, 1968).

Deist, W. *The Wehrmacht and German rearmament* (London, 1981): hardgoing but rewarding analysis of how the army viewed Hitler and his warlike policies.

Friedländer, S. *Prelude to downfall: Hitler and the United States 1939–1941* (London, 1967): largely neglected but a highly perceptive analysis of Hitler's changing attitude and policy towards the United States.

Gillingham, J.R. *Industry and politics in the Third Reich* (London, 1985).

Gorodetsky, G. *Grand Delusion: Stalin and the German Invasion of Russia* (Yale, 1999)

Hayes, P. *Industry and ideology: IG Farben in the Nazi era* (Cambridge, 1987): a masterly analysis demonstrating the complicity of the chemical combine.

Hildebrand, K. *The foreign policy of the Third Reich* (London, 1973).

James, H. *The German slump: politics and economics 1924–36* (Oxford, 1986): little on the Nazi wartime ecomomy but a first-rate analysis of the collapse of the German economy and the continuities and discontinuities in economic policy between Weimar and the Third Reich.

Kele, M.H. *Nazis and workers: national socialist appeals to German labor 1919–33* (Chapel Hill, N.C., 1972).

Mason, T.W. "Labour in the Third Reich", *Past and Present* (April, 1966), 112–41.

Mason, T.W. "The primacy of politics – politics and economics in national socialist Germany", in H. Turner (ed.) *Nazism and the Third Reich* (New York, 1972), 175–200.

Mason, T.W. "The workers' opposition in Nazi Germany", *History Workshop Journal* 11 (Spring, 1981), 120–37.

Mason, T.W. *Social policy in the Third Reich: the working class and the "National Community", 1918–39*, edited by J. Caplan (Oxford, 1992).

Milward, A.S. *The German economy at war* (London, 1965).

Müller, K.J. *Army, politics, and society in Germany 1933–45* (Manchester, 1984): a very important study.

Overy, R. "Hitler's war and the German economy: a reinterpretation", *Economic History Review* 35 (1982), 272–91: an impressive and persuasive demolition of Tim Mason's interpretation.

Overy, R. *The Nazi economic recovery 1932–38* (London, 1982).

Overy, R. *War and economy in the Third Reich* (Oxford, 1994): a collection of Overy's distinctive work on the Nazi economy.

Rich, N., *Hitler's war aims* (2 vols, London, 1973–4).

Robertson, E. *Hitler's pre-war policy and military plans* (London, 1983).

Sakwa, R. *The rise and fall of the USSR, 1917–1991* (London, forthcoming): the chapter on "The Road to Berlin, 1939–45" contains an excellent synthesis of recent Russian research on Stalin's foreign policy and his relationship with Hitler.

Salewski, M. & Schulze-Wegener, G. (eds) *Kriegsjahr 1944. Im Grossen und im Kleinen* (Stuttgart, 1995).

Schoenbaum, D. *Hitler's social revolution: class and status in Nazi Germany* (London, 1967): a groundbreaking interpretation in its day.

Schweitzer, A. *Big business in the Third Reich* (London, 1964).

Smelser, R. *Robert Ley: Hitler's labour front leader* (Oxford, 1988).

Taylor, A.J.P. *The origins of the Second World War* (London, 1961).

Turner, H.A. *German big business and the rise of Hitler* (Oxford, 1985): a very good overview of the relationship between leaders of business and Hitler.

Weinberg, G. *The foreign policy of Hitler's Germany: starting World War II* (London, 1980).

Weinberg, G. *Germany, Hitler and World War II* (Cambridge, 1995): an extremely valuable collection of over twenty essays.

Weinberg, G. (ed.) *Hitlers Zweites Buch. Ein Doikument aus dem Jahr 1928* (Stuttgart, 1961).

Weizsäcker, E. *The memoirs of Ernst von Weizsäcker* (London, 1951).

Racial policy, euthanasia and the "Jewish Question"

Aly, G. *"Endlösung"* (Frankfurt am Main, 1998).

Bankier, D. "Hitler and the policy-making process on the Jewish Question", *Holocaust and genocide studies* 3 (1988).

Bankier, D. *The Germans and the Final Solution: public opinion under Nazism* (London, 1992): a detailed and perceptive analysis.

Bartov, O. *The Eastern Front 1941–45: German troops and the barbarisation of warfare* (London, 1985).

Bauer, Y. *The Holocaust in historical perspective* (London, 1978).

BenGershom, E. *David: the testimony of a Holocaust survivor* (Oxford, 1988).

Browder, G. *Hitler's enforcers: the Gestapo and the SS Security Service in the Nazi revolution* (Oxford, 1997): a socio-organizational history that concentrates on the period 1932–7.

Breitman, R. *The architect of genocide: Himmler and the Final Solution* (London, 1991).

Browning, C. *Fateful months* (New York, 1985): a meticulous reconstruction of events that led to the implementation of the "Final Solution".

Browning, C. *The path to genocide: essays on launching the Final Solution* (Cambridge 1992)

Browning, C. *Ordinary men: reserve police battalion and the Final Solution in Poland* (London, 1992).

Burleigh, M. *Germany turns eastward: a study of Ostforschung in the Third Reich* (Cambridge, 1988).

Burleigh, M. "Surveys of developments in the social history of medicine: III. "Euthanasia" in the Third Reich: some recent literature", *The Society for the Social History of Medicine* (1991), 317–28.

Burleigh, M. *Death and deliverance: "euthanasia" in Germany 1900–45* (Cambridge, 1994).

Burleigh, M. & Wipperman, W. *The racial state: Germany 1933–1945* (Cambridge, 1991).

Burrin, P. *Hitler and the Jews: The genesis of the Holocaust* (London, 1994): a new and important synthesis.

Cesarani, D. (ed.) *The Final Solution: origins and implementation* (London, 1994) an excellent collection of essays to mark the fiftieth anniversary of the Wannsee Conference.

Dawidowicz, L. *The war against the Jews, 1933–45* (Harmondsworth, 1977).

Evans, R.T. *In Hitler's shadow* (New York/London, 1989).

Fleming, G. *Hitler and the Final Solution* (Oxford, 1986).

Gellately, R. *The Gestapo and German society: enforcing racial policy, 1933–1945* (Oxford, 1990): raises important issues of social complicity on the part of "ordinary" Germans.

Gerlach, C. "Die Wannsee-Konferenz, das Schicksal der deutschen Juden und Hitlers politische Grundsatzentscheidung, alle Juden Europas zu emorden", *Werkstatt Geschichte* 18 (November, 1997), 7–31.

Gerlach, C. "The Wannsee Conference, the Fate of German Jews, and Hitler's Decision in Principle to Exterminate All European Jews", *Journal of Modern History*, 70 (1988), 759–812.

Goldhagen, D. *Hitler's willing executioners: ordinary Germans and the Holocaust* (London, 1996).

Hilberg, R. *The destruction of European Jews* (New York, 1973).

Hirschfeld, G. (ed.) *The policies of genocide* (London, 1986).

Höhne, H. *The Order of the Death's Head* (London, 1972).

Kershaw, I. "Improvised genocide? The emergence of the 'Final Solution' in the 'Warthegau'", *Transactions of the Royal Historical Society* 2 (1992), 51–78.

Krausnick, H. & Broszat, M. *The anatomy of the SS State* (London, 1968): remains the standard work on the SS.

Maier, C. *The unmasterable past: history, Holocaust, and German national identity* (Cambridge, Mass., 1988).

Marrus, M. *The Holocaust in history* (London, 1988).

Mayer, A. *Why did the heavens not darken? The Final Solution in history* (New York, 1989).

Mommsen, H. *Beamtentum im Dritten Reich* (Stuttgart, 1966): the first statement of Hitler as a "weak dictator".

Mommsen, H. *From Weimar to Auschwitz* (Oxford, 1991): two very important chapters on Hitler's position within the Nazi system and the "realization of the unthinkable".

Mommsen, H. "Cumulative radicalization and progessive self-destruction as structural determinants of the Nazi dictatorship", in I. Kershaw and M. Lewin (eds) *Stalinism and Nazism: dictatorships in comparison* (London, 1997).

Müller-Hill, B. *Murderous science: elimination by scientific selection of Jews, Gypsies, and others: Germany 1933–45* (Oxford, 1988).

Pehle, W. (ed.) *November 1938: From the Reichskristallnacht to genocide* (Oxford, 1991).

Proctor, R.N. *Racial hygiene: medicine under the Nazis* (Cambridge, Mass., 1988).

Reitlinger, G. *The Final Solution* (London, 1953).

Schleunes, K.A. *The twisted road to Auschwitz: Nazi policy towards the Jews, 1933–39* (Chicago and London, 1970).

Stargardt, N. "The Holocaust" in M. Fulbrook (ed) *German History Since 1800* (London, 1997), 339–364.

Sternburg, W. von *Warum Wir? Die Deutschen und Der Holocaust* (Berlin, 1996).

Thomas, G. (ed.) *The unresolved past: a debate in German history*, intro. by R. Dahrendorf (London, 1990).

Wegner, B. *The Waffen SS: organization, ideology and function* (Oxford, 1990).

Weindling, P. *Health, race and German politics* (Cambridge, 1989).

Weinstein, F. *The dynamics of Nazism: leadership, ideology and the Holocaust* (London, 1980).

Welch, D. " 'Jews Out!' Anti-Semitic film propaganda in Nazi Germany and the 'Jewish Question' ", *The British Journal of Holocaust Education* vol. I, no. 1 (Summer 1992), 55–73.

General

Arendt, H. *The origins of totalitarianism* (New York, 1958).

Bessel, R. (ed.) *Life in the Third Reich* (Oxford, 1987): a valuable and wide-ranging selection of essays.

Broszat, M. *German national socialism* (Santa Barbara, Calif., 1966).

Broszat, M. *The Hitler State* (London, 1981): assesses Hitler's power and the structures within which he operated.

Burden, H.T. *The Nuremberg Rallies 1932–39* (London, 1967).

Bull, H. (ed.) *The challenge of the Third Reich* (Oxford, 1986).

Cecil, R. *Myth of the master race: A. Rosenberg and the Nazi ideology* (London, 1974).

Childers, T. & Caplan, J. (eds) *Re-evaluating the Third Reich* (New York, 1993): a "tired" collection of essays with the notable exception of Peter Hayes' contribution on economic policy and war, which I have quoted from in the text.

Ciano, G. *Ciano's diary, 1939–43* (London, 1947).

Conway, J.S. *The Nazi persecution of the churches 1933–45* (London, 1968).

Cuomo, G. (ed.) *Cultural policy of the national socialist regime* (New York, 1994).

Fröhlich, E. (ed.) *Die Tagebücher von Joseph Goebbels*, Part II: *Diktate 1941–1945* (Munich, 1993).

Glaser, H. *The cultural roots of national socialism* (London, 1978).

Grunberger, R. *A social history of the Third Reich* (London, 1974).

Hale, O.J. *The captive press in the Third Reich* (Princeton, 1964).

Heiber, H. (ed.) *Das Tagebuch von Joseph Goebbels 1925/26* (Stuttgart, 1960): translated as *The early Goebbels diaries: the journal of Joseph Goebbels from 1925–1926* (London, 1962).

Heiber, H. *Goebbels* (London, 1973).

Helmrich, E.C. *The German churches under Hitler* (Detroit, 1979).

Herzstein, R.E. *The war that Hitler won: the most infamous propaganda campaign in history* (London, 1979).

Hildebrand, K. *The Third Reich* (London, 1984).

Holborn, H. "Origins and Political Character of Nazi Ideology", *Political Science Quarterly*, LXXIX (1952) 542ff.

Joll, J. *Europe since 1870* (London, 1973).

Kershaw, I. "The persecution of the Jews and German popular opinion in the Third Reich", *Year Book of the Leo Baeck Institut* 26 (1981).

Keshaw, I. *Popular opinion and political dissent in the Third Reich* (Oxford, 1983).

Kershaw, I. "How effective was Nazi propaganda?", in D. Welch (ed.) *Nazi propaganda* (London, 1983), 180–205.

King, C. *The Nazi State and the new religions: five case studies in non-conformity* (New York/Toronto, 1982).

Koch, H.W. *The Hitler Youth: origins and development 1922–45* (London, 1975).

Koch, H.W. (ed.) *Aspects of the Third Reich* (London, 1985).

Koonz, C. "Mothers in the Fatherland: women in Nazi Germany", in R. Bridenthal, & C. Koonz (eds) *Becoming visible: women in European history* (Boston, 1977), 445–73.

Koonz, C. *Mothers in the Fatherland: women, the family, and Nazi Germany* (New York, 1987).

Khrushchev, N. *Khrushchev remembers* vol. 1 (London, 1971).

Large, D.C. (ed.) *Contending with Hitler: varieties of German resistance in the Third Reich* (Cambridge, Mass., 1991).

Lemmons, R. *Goebbels and "Der Angriff"* (Kentucky, 1994).

Lewy, G. *The Catholic church and Nazi Germany* (London, 1964).

Lochner, L.P. (ed.) *The Goebbels diaries* (London, 1948).

Longerich, P. *Hitlers Stellvertreter; Führung der Partei und Kontrolle des Staatsapparates durch Stab Hess die Partei-Kanzlei Bormann* (Munich, 1992): a very important "revisionist" work on the role of Bormann and his Party Chancellery; yet to be translated into English.

Mason, T.W. "Women in Germany, 1925–40: family, welfare and work", *History Workshop Journal* (Spring and Autumn 1976), 74–113; 5–32.

McIntyre, J. "Women and the professions in Germany 1930–40", in A. Nicholls & E. Mattias (eds) *German democracy and the triumph of Hitler* (London, 1971), 175–213.

Merkl, P. *Political violence under the swastika* (Princeton, 1975).

Merson, A. *Communist resistance in Nazi Germany* (London, 1987).

Mosse, G. *The crisis of German ideology: intellectual origins of the Third Reich* (London, 1964).

Mosse, G. *Nazi culture: intellectual, cultural and social life in the Third Reich* (London, 1966).

Neumann, F. *Behemoth: the structure and practice of national socialism* (London, 1942): dated, but still worth reading.

Nicosia, F. & Stokes, L. (eds) *Germans against Nazism: noncompliance, opposition and resistance in the Third Reich* (Oxford, 1990).

Peukert, D. *Inside Nazi Germany: conformity and opposition in everyday life* (London, 1987): tackles the question of coercion versus consensus.

Peukert, D. "Youth in the Third Reich", in R. Bessel (ed.) *Life in the Third Reich* (Oxford, 1987), 25–40.

Reimann, V. *Dr. Joseph Goebbels* (Vienna, 1973), translated as *The man who created Hitler* (London, 1977).

Reuth, R. G. *Goebbels* (New York, 1993).

Scholl, I. *Students against tyranny: the resistance of the White Rose, Munich 1942–43* (Middleton, Conn. 1983).

Semmler, R. *Goebbels: the man next to Hitler* (London, 1947).

Sereny, G. *Albert Speer: his battle with truth* (London, 1995).

Silfen, P.H. *The "völkisch" ideology and the roots of Nazism* (New York, 1973).

Speer, A. *Inside the Third Reich* (London, 1971).

Stern, F. *The politics of cultural despair: a study in the rise of the Germanic ideology* (Berkeley, 1961).

Stachura, P. *The German youth movement 1900–45* (London, 1981).

Stephenson, J. *Women in Nazi society* (London, 1975).

Stephenson, J. *The Nazi organisation of women* (London, 1981).

Taylor, F. (ed.) *The Goebbels diaries 1939–41* (London, 1982).

Taylor, R. *The word in stone: the role of architecture in the national Socialist ideology* (Berkeley and London, 1974).

Thies, J. "Hitler's European building programme", *Journal of Contemporary History* vol. 13 (1978), 413–31.

Trevor-Roper, H.R. (ed.)*The Goebbels diaries: the last days* (London, 1978).

Walker, L.D. *Hitler youth and Catholic youth 1933–36* (Washington, 1971).

Welch, D. *Propaganda and the German cinema 1933–45* (Oxford, 1983): deals with the way in which Hitler was portrayed in the Nazi cinema.

Welch, D. "Nazi wartime newsreel propaganda", in K. Short (ed.) *Film and radio propaganda in World War II: a global perspective* (London, 1983), 201–19.

Welch, D. (ed.) *Nazi propaganda: the power and the limitations* (London, 1983).

Welch, D. "Propaganda and indoctrination in the Third Reich: success or failure?", *European History Quarterly* vol. 17 (October, 1987), 403–22.

Welch, D. "Goebbels, Götterdämmerung, and the Deutsche Wochenschauen", in K. Short & S. Dolezel (eds) *Hitler's fall: the newsreel witness* (London, 1988).

Welch, D. "Manufacturing a consensus: Nazi propaganda and the building of a national community", *Contemporary European History* vol. 2, no. 1 (1993), 1–15.

Welch, D. *Modern European history, 1871–2000: a documentary reader* (London, 1999).

Welch, D. *The Third Reich: politics and propaganda* (London, 1993; all references to 2nd edn 1995).

Wykes, A. *The Nuremberg Rallies* (New York, 1970).

Index

921
Hit

Welch, David,
1950-

Hitler.

DATE			
2/19/03			